A POCKET GUIDE TO ANALYZING FILMS

A POCKET GUIDE TO ANALYZING FILMS

Robert Spadoni

UNIVERSITY OF CALIFORNIA PRESS

University of California Press, one of the most distinguished university presses in the United States, enriches lives around the world by advancing scholarship in the humanities, social sciences, and natural sciences. Its activities are supported by the UC Press Foundation and by philanthropic contributions from individuals and institutions. For more information, visit www.ucpress.edu.

University of California Press
Oakland, California

Frontispiece: *Double Indemnity* (Billy Wilder, 1944).

Library of Congress Cataloging-in-Publication Data

Spadoni, Robert, 1964–.
    A pocket guide to analyzing films / Robert Spadoni.
        pages cm
    Includes index.
    ISBN 978-0-520-28069-4 (cloth : alk. paper)
    ISBN 978-0-520-28070-0 (pbk. : alk. paper)
    ISBN 978-0-520-95876-0 (e-book)
    1. Film criticism.   I. Title.
    PN1995.s6115 2014
    791.4301'5—dc23
                                2014005896

Manufactured in China

23 22 21 20 19 18 17 16 15 14
10 9 8 7 6 5 4 3 2 1

The paper used in this publication meets the minimum requirements of ANSI/NISO Z39.48–1992 (R 2002) (Permanence of Paper).

FOR DIANA

CONTENTS

ACKNOWLEDGMENTS

Great film teachers who have inspired me include Antonia Lant, the late Robert Sklar, and especially Tom Gunning, whose brilliance and passion continue to set the bar for my highest aspirations in the classroom. A legendary teacher I never took a class with is Louis Giannetti, who taught film studies at Case Western in the years before my coming and who, when I got here, generously shared teaching tips and techniques with me that he'd honed over three decades. The lessons, philosophies, and enthusiasm of these mentors have gone into this book, as has the ongoing enrichment I gain from my students. At Case Western, thanks to my colleagues in the English Department and to William Claspy and Gayle Spinazze. At the University of California Press, thanks to Rachel Berchten, Sandy Drooker, Kim Hogeland, and especially Mary Francis, for her encouragement, guidance, and wonderful editorial eye. I'm grateful to the anonymous readers for their helpful comments, Rick Worland for his insights and advice, and Joe Abbott for his copyediting. Thanks to my parents, Norma and Ed Spadoni, for finding my author photo in the attic and for everything else they've done. To my children, Nora, Louise, and Matilda, thanks for making the world go round, and an extra hug goes to Nora for proofreading the manuscript. Finally, Diana Simeon supported the making of this book in so many ways. To her I express my deepest love and gratitude.

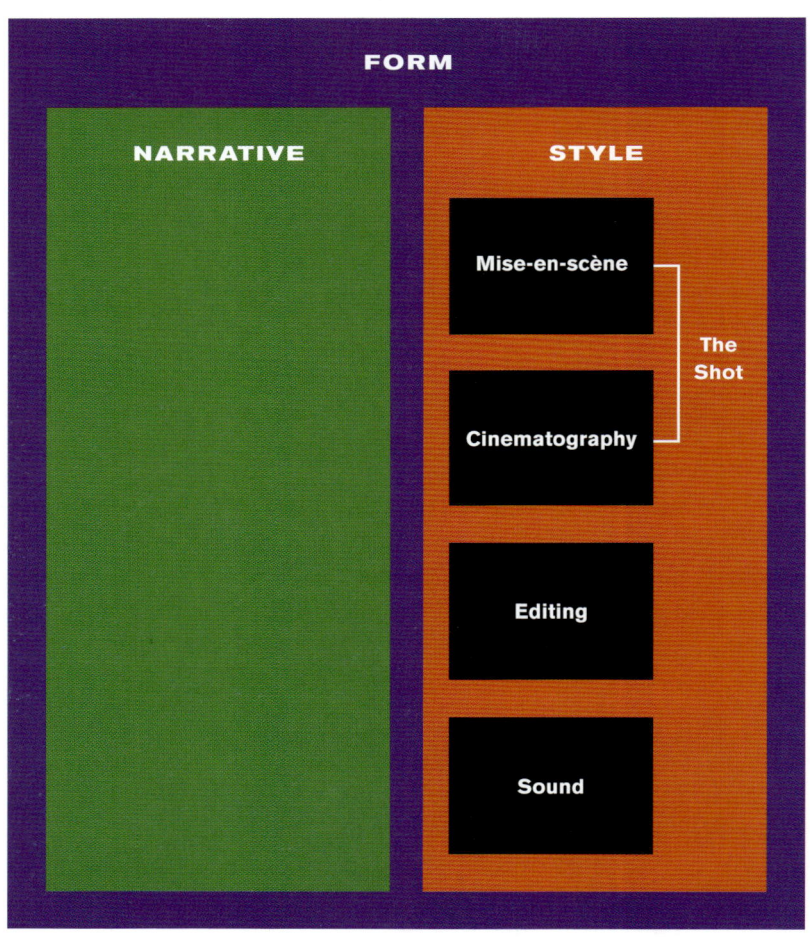

The major components of a narrative film.

Introduction

A Pocket Guide to Analyzing Films is founded on the belief that most any film can be better understood and appreciated when it is viewed as a system in which the parts relate to each other and together make up the whole. Thinking about a film in this way is sometimes called "close reading" and sometimes "textual analysis." We will call it **formal analysis.**

Because it focuses exclusively on describing the methods of formal analysis, and on making a case for their usefulness regardless of one's specific interest in the cinema, this book leaves out a lot of things. It concentrates on those aspects of the film-viewing experience that don't change, or have changed the least, over time. There's nothing, or close to it, on silent versus sound cinema, IMAX, Technicolor, YouTube, and 3-D. And there's a minimum on how techniques are executed, on behind-the-scenes production realities like optical printers, performance capture suits, Final Cut Pro, and stunt doubles. The focus, instead, is on the *results* of these efforts, what happens on the screen, the functions and effects of these techniques both individually and, more important, when they work together. There is little mention of the turn to digital cinema in recent years, because the thing that we'll be calling "film form" has not been remade by this change. The methods, terminology, and target of the kind of analysis described in this book have not experienced the upheavals currently sweeping the world's cinema institutions, technologies, and economies. There's no overview of the movie business today or even a snapshot of movie history. And this isn't a how-to guide for aspiring filmmakers. That said, filmmakers who want to learn more about how films shape the viewing experience will find here a concise road map to the tools and principles that govern this dynamic and richly complex process.

The key word is *concise*. This *Pocket Guide* is designed to be just that, small enough to have with you whenever and wherever you might need it, both in and out of class. What it lacks in breadth and depth, I hope it makes up for with portability. Provided is only what you'll need to be able to sift through the elements that make up a film, regardless of your particular interest or orientation to it. Your interest might be in learning more about how films cohere and work their effects. Or maybe you have a more focused goal. You might be taking a course in film theory (classical, semiotic, or cognitivist, for example), or on a genre (science fiction, musicals, film noir, etc.), or a survey of movie history, or a course on race and gender in film, the French New Wave, cinemas of the Pacific Rim, Alfred Hitchcock, film adaptation, or any of a hundred other possibilities. Such a course will expose you to readings that will help you explore its specific topical material. But the heart of your inquiry, regardless of the course focus, will be films. This book, as much as possible, cuts across historical and national boundaries, driving at all times toward the common core of elements that make up films of virtually every kind. Here are the specialized terms and concepts that you will need to make formal analysis the robust center of a persuasive film essay.

Described are not only film techniques but also more general ideas that will help you make sense of those techniques. You notice that a shot is filmed from a low angle. Why should you or anyone else care? A major reason is that you can organize things like camera angles into patterns that will help you ask, and answer, "big questions" about a film, including what it means. More valuable than helping you *articulate* what you think is going on in a film, these principles can help you *discover* what is going on. Most of these principles are described in part 1, in chapter 1, the longest and most important chapter in the book.

The images in this book are digital captures from films, not production stills, which are photographs taken on the film set for promotional purposes and not accurate representations of how the film looks on the screen. You'll also find thumbnail readings of a selection of films and film sequences, pointers on writing a film essay, and notes on areas of possible confusion—like terms that sound alike but mean different things, and ones that mean similar or overlapping things. I try to clear these up as I go. I urge you to flag them with your pen or highlighter as you go.

My advice, unless your teacher instructs you otherwise, is to read this book all the way through once, marking it up, making it yours. It's short and has lots of pictures, so this should not be a difficult task. Then have it with you when you watch a film, and keep it handy afterward when you're looking at your viewing notes, making your outline, drafting your essay, and going back to the film. Filmmakers have at their disposal an amazingly powerful tool kit for putting a film together. Most every task and problem they encounter can be handled in a wide variety of ways. Filmmakers have, above all, a range of choices for construing and meeting the creative challenges they face. *And something is always gained or lost when one choice is favored over another.* This book is about the choices and about how you can examine them in a way that will help you more fully grasp and appreciate how they all come together.

This book is indebted to the work of David Bordwell and Kristin Thompson, whose *Film Art: An Introduction* carries on and consolidates the long tradition, in film studies, of closely examining individual films. This tradition includes writing by such major figures as French film critic André Bazin and Soviet filmmaker and theorist Sergei Eisenstein, both of whom I briefly consider in the pages that follow. But it is Bordwell and Thompson who lay out what has become the standard approach to the formal analysis of films. This *Pocket Guide* gratefully acknowledges their foundational contribution to the discipline.

Some final notes. First, this book can help you analyze many kinds of films, including experimental and documentary films, but the emphasis is on story films. Second, while this book can help readers interested in any national cinema, the majority of films referenced are U.S. films. And finally, at the first mention of a film, the producing country is given only when it is not the United States.

FORM

This first part of the book isn't really about film. There is little in it about the medium, not much on specific techniques of storytelling, cinematography, editing, and so on. All of that starts with part 2. But this part is crucial. It lays out the core ideas of the approach this book takes to analyzing films. The focus of part 1, consisting of chapter 1, is the concept of form in artworks. You'll use the ideas in this chapter as a framework that the rest of the chapters in this book will fit inside.

Film as Form

What is form? Think of **form** as the way the different parts of an artwork relate to each other and how they come together to make up the whole. We are conceiving of the artwork as a *system*.

This book has two major emphases. One is analyzing a film *as a film*, really digging into the particulars of what makes it a film versus being a work in another medium, such as literature or theater. The second emphasis *is seeing the whole in terms of the parts and seeing the parts in terms of the whole.* There's a half-hour French film titled *La jetée* (Chris Marker, 1962) that consists almost entirely of still images. Only a single shot, lasting six seconds, contains movement in the sense of what we understand a motion picture to do most fundamentally. In it a woman blinks her eyes. It's a moment that can leave a viewer moved and even awestruck. Suppose you told your friend, "I saw this movie last night, and there was a scene where a woman blinks her eyes, and her eyes *actually move!* It was awesome." Your friend would look at you as though you were crazy. The point is that the extraordinary thing about this moment only makes sense if you look at it in the context of the whole film. Looking at the whole film in terms of its parts involves grounding your analysis in the concrete specifics of the film you are examining.

This book describes a way of looking at films, an approach and a philosophy, and everything in it turns on this idea of form.

People enjoy seeing how the parts of something fit together. In *Star Wars: Episode IV—A New Hope* (George Lucas, 1977) Han Solo comes flying out of nowhere and blasts Darth Vader's ship, giving Luke Skywalker a clear shot at destroying the Death Star. But, of course, Han doesn't really come out of nowhere. We know this character. We've seen him before. We like him. The film has coaxed us temporarily to forget about him, but when he returns, it's like the pleasurable feeling one experiences when a jigsaw puzzle piece drops into place. The character belongs there. The parts fit together. This is form.

Now, if people enjoy artworks that convey a sense of themselves as robustly complete, a film can tap into this desire and satisfy it. A film that does this is *The Sixth Sense* (M. Night Shyamalan, 1999), when, in the final minutes, the whole film snaps into a new and super-crisp focus. We learn something that assigns new meanings to almost everything that has come before. The film turns out to have a tighter organization, to be more systematic, than we thought. If people love this film, this is a big reason why.

But a filmmaker can *frustrate* this desire as well, in ways that can be just as interesting and worthwhile as the happiest ending of the most mainstream blockbuster movie. Both kinds of film exhibit form equally, and both kinds will reward close study.

A VIEWER-CENTERED APPROACH

A common way to understand form is to set it off against "content." The form/content distinction is so widespread in discussions of films and other artworks that many people take it as a given. But, while some academic writing and other serious discussions make this distinction, I am going to suggest that there are benefits to putting it aside and understanding form in an entirely different way.

Refraining from discussing content won't limit us in what we can say about a film. This is because anything a person might call "content" will be something we'll include in our discussion of form. Suppose by "content" someone means a film's story. A little man with big hairy feet goes on a journey to destroy an evil ring. That's content. But we're going to call that *narrative,* the topic of the next chapter, where we'll view narrative as deeply and inextricably a part of form. Others might mean *subject matter,* World War I, say. But everything in a film that might *represent* this subject matter—costumes, trenches, guns, dialogue, even archival footage of the actual war—will all be things that we will identify as elements of form. World War I isn't "inside" this film, isn't a part of it, any more than Middle Earth is inside Peter Jackson's *Lord of the Rings* trilogy or J. R. R. Tolkien's books are inside it. The same real-world event or work of literature can inspire many films, but these films won't all share a common core material that is a war or a book. And finally, what if by *content* someone means *meaning*? This chapter will have a lot to say about meaning, but for now I'll just say that we won't be calling it content.

It's all form—which is good, because this means that nothing in a film is outside the scope of your analysis. Well, there are three other things, besides content, that I will suggest you can fruitfully avoid when analyzing a film. We get to these later in the chapter. But first, if we're not understanding form by opposing it to content, how are we understanding it?

We'll see a strong relationship between form and *expectations*. Whose? Those of viewers. There are many kinds of approach to film analysis. Here you'll learn about one that is *formalist* and also *viewer centered*. Another kind is author centered, which we will consider briefly when we get to films and *function* later in the chapter.

Broadly speaking, viewer expectations can come from two places: (1) the work itself, the film; and (2) outside the film, our daily experiences, including our experience of watching other films.

If I say "knock knock," you'll say, "Who's there?" You can participate in the joke—you can, in a sense, help make it "happen"—because you've heard other knock-knock jokes and know what to say. This knowledge is external to the joke and helps you make sense of it. In fact, without this knowledge there is no joke at all.

Now, if in answer to your "Who's there?" I say, "Cash," and you say, "Cash who?" and I say, "No thanks, but I'd like some peanuts," your expectation—that "Cash" is at the door—comes not from past experiences but from the joke itself.

The joke *cued* you to have this expectation.

The interplay between these two kinds of expectation, ones coming from outside the text and ones coming from inside it, is something you can look for and ask questions about when watching a film.

More about the expectations we bring to films. You go to a musical. You expect to see people breaking into song and dance as you don't in life. If you've never seen a musical before, your reaction might not be, "Oh, they're falling in love," but, "What's happening? I don't get this at all." Again, what viewers know coming to a film plays a role in helping to make the film "happen."

Viewer expectations will be part of our understanding of form and of what films are and what they do.

CONVENTIONS AND GENRES

One way film form and viewer expectations interact is through *conventions*. A **convention** is a trait that is shared by many artworks and that we don't see, or see nearly as often, in real life. Viewers are able to understand a convention in part because they've seen it before in other films. For this reason, we can think about a convention as a way films relate, through viewers, to other films.

The number of film conventions one could list is endless. Here are four:

- A man and woman meet and instantly hate each other. If this is a romantic comedy, they'll probably fall in love.
- The mad genius doesn't get away with his diabolical scheme.
- The car explodes in slow motion.
- The underdog sports team comes from behind at the last second and wins the big game.

Another way to understand conventions is to say they can help us distinguish movie reality from actual reality. Consider the ticking-time-bomb scenario. A captured suspect possesses some secret information, and if his interrogators can only find it out—under what bridge the bomb is wired, say—many innocent lives will be saved. If it's hard to find examples of a time when such a scenario ever played out in real life, it happens every week on TV and in one big-screen action thriller after another. The scenario belongs more to movie reality than to the one we live in. In real life, if two people meet and instantly hate each other, chances are they'll just go on hating each other.

As many of my examples suggest, conventions can point strongly to certain types of films. If you're watching a film featuring a protagonist, maybe a private investigator, who's visited by a sultry woman who asks for his help and who might be secretly treacherous, you're probably watching a film noir (or a parody of one). Film noir is an example of a **film genre.** Most moviegoers are familiar with genres of many kinds—action-adventure, romantic comedy, westerns, and so on. Conventions can be spotted in every kind of film, but genre films are loaded with them to distinctive degrees. Let's consider an example.

In the science fiction film *The Matrix* (Andy Wachowski and Lana Wachowski, US/Australia, 1999), the hero, Neo, decides to face the evil Agent Smith. The scene is a deserted subway. Trinity, the female protagonist, who loves Neo, has just made her narrow escape. She is no wallflower, but the telephone link that would allow her to return to his side has just been severed. It's a convention of many kinds of film that the hero must face his nemesis alone. Obi-Wan's ghost, in *Star Wars: Episode V—The Empire Strikes Back* (Irvin Kershner, 1980), tells Luke: "If you choose to face Vader, you will do it alone. I cannot interfere." One could argue that the rules of movie showdowns between good and bad guys govern Obi-Wan's exclusion from this confrontation as much as any logic internal to the Star Wars universe does. Likewise excluded, Trinity urges, "Run, Neo, run." The woman, helpless on the sidelines, fears for her man's safety. But he's going to stand firm. That this scenario is far from original makes it no less compelling.

When Neo doesn't run, Trinity asks his mentor, Morpheus, "What's he doing?" Morpheus replies, "He's beginning to believe." Viewers feel a surge of gratification as well as anticipation at this line. Since long before Harry Potter, Luke Skywalker, and the cinema itself, the protagonist

1.1 *The Matrix.* Hero and villain square off in a classic western gunfight configuration.

who turns out to be, at the moment of truth, The One has been a staple of many kinds of story.

Then the two face off, and the invocation of genre conventions becomes more explicit. The camera shoots past the hips and hands first of Smith and then of Neo (**1.1**). This is a subway, not a street in a western, but the newspaper pages blowing past call tumbleweeds to mind with enough vividness to clinch the association. Without breaking the dramatic tension, the film has placed us in the O.K. Corral. The shots of ready fingers inches from triggers, the stillness of the moment just before the gunslingers draw, the tumbleweed-like trash—all of this is **genre iconography,** which is imagery (or sounds) we recognize from one genre film to the next that both helps to make the films more meaningful and coherent and helps to bind the genre together. Swinging saloon doors, space helmets, full moons accompanied by howling wolves, and action heroes coolly walking toward the camera in slow motion while something big explodes in the background are all examples of genre iconography.

The sequence continues to unspool a tissue of conventions and spin them into new combinations, from the "bullet time" slow-motion special effect (new in 1999 but now a convention, and even cliché, of films and video games) to, when the two finally land, both learning at the same time that their guns are empty. Then hand-to-hand combat ensues, and the acrobatic fighting sparks connections to Asian martial arts cinema, a genre to which the film owes an undisguised debt.

To sum up, film form relates to viewer expectations, and infiltrating both expectations and form, in genre and other sorts of films, are conventions.

THREE KINDS OF RESPONSE

Form also bears on viewer emotions. Of the different sorts of feelings a viewer might experience while watching a film, one is **curiosity.** Someone in a film is carrying a box. The other characters are greatly interested in its contents. We might be inclined to wonder what's in the box, to feel curious.

When thinking about how films cue us to experience emotions, it's tempting, and often productive, to look at the emotions the characters are experiencing and to ask how we're being encouraged to mirror these feelings. Such a response is a function of the extent to which we **identify** with the characters as they (and we) move through a story. But viewers respond to the whole film, not just the characters, and our emotional experiences can differ greatly from those of the characters, even ones we care about deeply. Returning to the box scenario, maybe all the characters know what's in the box, but we don't. So our curiosity is not theirs. This is important because, again, we want to think about how the whole film is cueing us to experience emotions and not just how the characters are doing it.

Curiosity is one response. We'll spend more time considering two others: *suspense* and *surprise*. These terms can help you think in precise ways about how films shape the viewing experience from moment to moment.

Suspense hinges on a delay in an outcome we are anticipating. The film makes us wait for what we think, and sometimes are pretty sure, is going to happen. Will James Bond defuse the bomb? Probably, and he does, but not until the last five minutes of the film. In the meantime we

1.2 *Indiana Jones and the Temple of Doom*. Has Indy made it?

1.3 Yes he has.

feel emotionally connected to the story. Suspense is a powerful means by which films elicit our emotional involvement.

In contrast to suspense, **surprise** results when a film leads us to expect one thing and something else happens instead.

With these two terms in mind, let's turn to some films. Which would you use to characterize this moment in *Indiana Jones and the Temple of Doom* (Steven Spielberg, 1984)? The rope bridge across the chasm has snapped, a terrific hand-to-hand battle has ensued on the dangling bridge, and all the bad guys have fallen into the river—but has Indy survived? The camera lingers on the empty frame (**1.2**). Then Indy's hand slowly comes into view as he climbs up, and then we see that in his other hand he holds the sacred stone he has recovered from the vanquished evil cult (**1.3**).

Let's look at how this sequence elicits suspense:

- We see an empty frame, with much of the visual field out of focus. We're used to watching films with people front and center, and in focus, so this image, on this basic level, is priming us to expect that something, probably our hero, will imminently come into view.

- Viewers who've seen *Raiders of the Lost Ark* (Spielberg, 1981) know that *Temple of Doom* is a prequel. They know Indy has further adventures, so they expect him to have survived this battle on the bridge.

- Even viewers who haven't seen *Raiders* know that *Temple of Doom* is an adventure story featuring a bigger-than-life hero who survives one perilous scrape after another. We know that these kinds of heroes in these kinds of films tend to prevail and that the one in this film probably will as well.

Our expectations are satisfied, but we have to wait. This is suspense.

Now consider this German TV commercial for a caffeinated beverage. To tranquil music the camera glides right as it follows a car moving in the same direction on the road below. In the first image the car is about to go behind a tree (**1.4**). The car disappears and the camera continues moving to the right, but then the music is abruptly replaced by a shriek as a figure bolts into view from the opposite direction (**1.5**).

Let's consider how this commercial elicits surprise:

- Placid music accompanies the gliding rightward movement of the camera as we watch, on a distant green landscape that's in focus, a car moving in the same direction.

- When the car goes behind a tree, we expect it to come out the other side.

- Instead, we're confronted with several sharp contrasts. A figure, not far away and in focus but very close and out of focus, enters the frame moving right to left, which jolts us, as we've been

1.4 TV ad for "K-Fee Turbo-drink." The car is about to go behind a tree.

1.5 Instead of the car emerging from the other side, this figure darts in from the right.

following the camera's and car's left-to-right movement. And instead of placid music, we have the incredibly loud shriek of this ghoulish figure.

• This commercial imitates conventions of car commercials we've seen before. One might have been waiting for a voice to say something about excellent gas mileage and expert road handling. This miniature film has tapped into our prior experiences to knock us off guard.

A final example comes from a scene in *Pulp Fiction* (Quentin Tarantino, 1994). Vincent Vega is a character in this anthology of three stories that all take place at the same time and in the same milieu, and with, up to this point, only minimal and inconsequential overlappings of characters

1.6 *Pulp Fiction.* Butch finds the gun.

1.7 Vincent comes out of the bathroom.

and events across the stories. We've seen the segment featuring Vincent. Now we're watching the one featuring Butch Coolidge, who, even though he knows gunmen are after him, has returned to his residence to retrieve a prized possession.

Butch finds a gun on his kitchen counter (**1.6**). Then he hears a toilet flush behind him. Vincent comes out of the bathroom (**1.7**). A tense moment follows, after which Butch mows Vincent down.

Let's look at this sequence in light of our two terms:

- By keeping the segments mostly insulated from one another, the film has led us to expect that there won't be major convergences of plotlines and characters across the stories. We're surprised by this confrontation and its violent outcome. Who would expect Vincent to be in the bathroom, and, even more shocking, to die? This isn't even his story!

- We came to know and like Vincent in the segment featuring him. And now we like Butch and are rooting for him. The film has taken a major character from another story and suddenly planted him in this story, running one protagonist right up against another. How do we feel? Is Vincent now the bad guy? That seems wrong. Should Butch die? That would be terrible. Viewers are caught in a carefully laid and, compared to the way most narrative films work, unusual trap. The rareness of the situation helps to make it all the more unexpected.

- We feel surprise. However, once the characters face off, the sequence becomes charged with an emotion of a different kind. Now viewers are burning with a single question: will Butch kill Vincent? We wait. This is suspense. The toaster pastry Butch popped in before he found the gun, and which we've forgotten about, springs up just before the gun fires, functioning simultaneously as a little surprise dotting the scene and, when it ejects from the toaster (with its built-in timer), as a reminder that the waiting interval it punctuates has been thick with an atmosphere of suspense.

There are as many kinds of emotional response as there are individual viewers and individual moments in films, but curiosity, suspense, and surprise are three kinds you will encounter often.

MEANING

Another way viewers respond to films is to find meaning in them. Film students do as well, but here the activity you'll be engaging in will be different from that of a casual viewer. To write a film essay is to enter into a relationship with a film that is more creative, and more aggressive, than when you're watching a film just for enjoyment and to find out what happens. Sorting elements of the film into categories and looking for patterns, asking questions that would only occur to someone on a second or third viewing, coming up with an argument—which is a story of sorts but one that differs from any the film might be telling—all of this is an activity that we differentiate from casual viewing and that we call **interpretation.**

Mounting a convincing film interpretation is an exciting and challenging task. A hurdle you'll face is that the case you're making can come across to your reader as abstract, vague, and impressionistic. Someone might read your analysis and say, "That's just what you think. Why should I believe you?" The questions for us, then, become: How do I make a case for film meaning that goes beyond mere opinion? How do I write an interpretation in such a way that, although there will always be room for disagreement and differing views, my arguments will seem concrete and persuasive? How do I ground the claims I'm making in the film itself?

We can start by understanding that by "meaning," it's possible to mean different things. In *Film Art,* David Bordwell and Kristin Thompson note that we can speak about four levels of meaning: *referential meaning, explicit meaning, implicit meaning,* and *symptomatic meaning.* We'll begin with the most concrete level and work our way down.

Referential Meaning

Referential meaning is a summary of a film's plot. It's everything the film visibly and audibly presents to us. Note that even at this topmost level, meaning can be unclear and contested. Suppose a character in a film mails a letter. The referential meaning of the blue metal box the character puts the letter inside is that it's a mailbox. But what if I come from a country where the mailboxes are yellow and shaped like tubes? I might not understand the referential meaning of the blue metal box. Or consider the last image in *Inception* (Christopher Nolan, US/UK, 2010): a spinning top. To some viewers this image reveals that everything that has come before, including the parts of the film where the characters are supposed to be awake, is a dream. Others might not read the image this way, and to these viewers *Inception* has a different referential meaning.

As these examples suggest, referential meaning, rather than being "contained" in a film, is something that *arises in the encounter between the film and its viewer.* You might not be accustomed to thinking about this sort of thing as meaning, but it's helpful to do so because it reminds us that *all* meaning is constructed, a negotiation between the artwork and its perceiver, and not something "immanent" or built into the work. As a film cues us to experience, say, suspense, so it does to construe referential meaning.

One might describe the referential meaning of *Groundhog Day* (Harold Ramis, 1993) as follows: a man keeps waking up on the same day and reliving it until he learns to be a better person.

Explicit Meaning

Explicit meaning is the level at which one would expect to find a film's message or moral or point. An explicit meaning of a film about a man who robs banks and goes to prison might be *Crime doesn't pay.* In *Groundhog Day* someone talking to Phil, the character caught in the time loop, says, "I bet you is a glass-is-half-empty kind of guy, is that right?" Based on this line, one might be inspired to describe an explicit meaning of the film as *Be a glass-is-half-full kind of person.* This is one possibility. As with most films, there are many ways one could construe and articulate explicit meaning in this one.

Implicit Meaning

More abstract and "below the surface" than explicit meaning, **implicit meaning** affords more room for disagreement and competing claims. Here is an example of implicit meaning. It's possible to see *Groundhog Day* as a movie about movies, with Phil trapped in a kind of "closed set"

1.8 *Trouble in Paradise.* The delayed appearance of "Paradise" . . .

1.9 . . . slyly invites viewers to read an implicit meaning in this title sequence.

where, because he knows everything that's going to happen next, he sounds like the director—as when, watching a street scene, he says, "A dog barks, cue the truck, exit Herman." Or maybe he sounds like someone who has seen a movie hundreds of times and knows every line of dialogue by heart. Also, the string of times Phil steps into, or avoids stepping into, the puddle on the street looks like a film's outtakes (or gag) reel. To someone interpreting the film along these lines, the scene in which Phil dresses up like Clint Eastwood in a spaghetti western and goes to the movies takes on special significance. It would be hard to argue that this throwaway scene strikes many viewers as the most important one in the film, but you might save it for the end of your essay, where you're trying to bring the case you're making about implicit meaning to as persuasive a close as you can.

One can speak about implicit meaning in relation to a whole film or just to a specific moment in one. As *Trouble in Paradise* (Ernst Lubitsch, 1932) begins, the elements of the title screen materialize in this order: first "Trouble in"; then the background image (**1.8**); then, following a pause, "Paradise" (**1.9**). The sequence gives us plenty of time, before the last word appears, to contemplate a possible implicit meaning, which is that this film is really going to be about trouble in the bedroom.

We have been talking about *levels* of meaning. Here's where it can get tricky. We can also speak about the *kinds* of meaning one finds on these levels. For referential meaning the kind of meaning is a film's *plot* (more on this word is in chapter 2). For explicit and implicit meanings the kind is *themes*. With this in mind let's turn to the fourth, and in some ways most complex, level of meaning.

Symptomatic Meaning

Symptomatic meaning absorbs the other three levels. It incorporates a film's story as well as what it seems to be trying to say.

Symptomatic meaning is a level of meaning. A *kind* of meaning one finds at this level is **ideology,** which means social values. These are the beliefs a culture holds, and often takes for granted, possibly so completely that these values are seldom examined or even acknowledged. They can even be unconscious. And yet the culture produces these artifacts—magazine ads, TV shows, clothing fashions, films—and in these artifacts we find these values embedded and expressed, sometimes inadvertently. These are things a film is "saying" without necessarily knowing or caring that it's saying them.

What kinds of things? It can vary tremendously, but when thinking about symptomatic meaning, it's helpful to remember what we typically mean by a "symptom." No one ever goes to a doctor and says, "When I raise my arm like this, it feels great!" A symptom is usually a sign that something is off, suspicious, fishy. So a symptomatic meaning in a film would probably not be *Always tell the truth*. More likely, one would find that message at the explicit level.

1.10 *Groundhog Day.* Rita, having purchased Phil, reaches up to claim and rescue him.

At the end of *Groundhog Day,* when Phil has learned his lesson, his love interest, Rita, "buys him" at a fund-raising auction (**1.10**). She wears party attire that, one could argue, is on the masculine side: trousers, a plain white blouse, and a vest. Meanwhile, Phil is onstage being ogled and hungrily bid on by the women in the room. This appears to be a reversal of what one finds in many Hollywood films, where the man takes the active role and "wins" the woman, who typically is the one standing on the pedestal and serving as the object of admiring male eyes. In this fairy tale, however, *Rita* breaks the spell, and *Phil* is the Snow White or Sleeping Beauty figure.

Is this film suggesting that to become a better man, Phil must become more like a woman? Rita, from the moment we first see her, is virtuous, content, and kind. She doesn't need to change her relationship to the world at all. Phil is the one with the problems. Maybe his main problem is that he's a man and stereotypically male in the way he schemes to seduce women, thinks only of himself, and acts nice only when he's being superficial and devious. This isn't a sexist view of the kind most commonly encountered in a film, but we might call it sexist all the same.

Someone interpreting the film along *these* lines might focus on the scene in which Phil's cameraman, Larry, sits at a bar and tries a lame pickup line on a woman, and the bartender, wiping a glass, shoots him

1.11 The bartender smiles at Larry's attempt to impress a woman.

1.12 Earlier, he smiled at Phil's attempt to impress Rita.

a knowing look (**1.11**). The moment strongly recalls an earlier scene in which Phil, conniving to put his powers to selfish advantage, tries a lame line on Rita, and the bartender, wiping a glass, shoots him a nearly identical look (**1.12**). Also growing salient within this interpretation, and a good candidate for a moment to save for last in an essay making *this* argument, is the scene in which Rita lists the qualities her idea of a perfect man would possess, and Phil quips, "This is a *man* we're talking about, right?"

I want to spend more time on symptomatic meaning because it can be both a difficult level to understand and an especially rich one to mine. One can view ideology expressed at this level as a value that has been presumed to constitute a common ground between a film's makers and its viewers. If it's totally shared, it can be totally invisible. This can mean the difference between a comedy being funny or just offensive. (And the complexities of viewer response are suggested in the fact that a comedy can be both these things at the same time.) When a gap opens up between the values a film seems to be presuming its viewers will hold and the ones they actually hold, symptomatic meanings can surge into view.

Endings can be good places to look for symptomatic meanings because it's here that a film is often striving, and sometimes straining, for maximum viewer satisfaction, maximum common ground. At the end of *Indiana Jones and the Temple of Doom* the female love interest, Willie, defiantly tells Indy that she's not going with him on any more adventures and storms off. A loud crack is heard, and we next see her wrapped around the waist with Indy's trademark whip (**1.13**). He reels her in and cinches her close for a kiss (**1.14**).

What observations can we make about symptomatic meanings in this scene?

- Willie asserts her independence when she breaks away from Indy and insists that she's not going with him to Delhi.

- Like she's an ornery cow or an unbroken filly, Indy "lassos" her and ropes her in.

- And she likes it. The goal of the filmmakers is surely not to spur angry reflections on gender roles in society, Hollywood cinema, and this film. The goal is to make us cheer the scene and feel happy. What values does the film seem to be presuming we'll share with it? Possibly these: *Women like a strong man, right? The kind who takes charge, and orders for both himself and the lady at restaurants. And girls, that Harrison Ford is handsome, isn't he? See how he cocks his hat back and grins like a lovable scoundrel? Who wouldn't go to Delhi with him in a heartbeat! And guys, wouldn't you like to have the unshaven good looks and general wherewithal to get the girl just like that, every time, no questions asked?*

1.13 Indy prevents Willie from leaving.

1.14 They embrace.

At a screening I once attended of this film, the audience loudly booed this scene. The "feel good" calculations of the filmmakers, for this crowd at least, missed their mark by a wide measure.

Someone who objects to picking apart so harmless an entertainment as an Indiana Jones movie might mount a defense along these lines: What about the argument that the film is looking back to an earlier time in American cinema and society? It's a nostalgic film, winking at us as it evokes the conventions, styles, and beliefs of a more innocent era. The sexist overtones of the sequence should be viewed in this light.

In response to this argument I would ask, What if Indy's sidekick, Short Round, had been, instead of an Asian boy, an African American in the mold of the Stepin Fetchit character seen in Hollywood films of decades past? What if he was a lazy, slow-witted, drawling, shiftless, bumbling, obsequious racist stereotype? What if, as with many African American characters (inevitably minor and comical) in these films, he was constantly dropping Indy's suitcases and hightailing it out of sight at every first sign of danger? If this character would be unthinkable in a film today, why is the stereotype of the uppity girlfriend who just needs to be knocked into line okay?

Some might insist that the sequence is less problematic than I claim, but this is the nature of analysis and interpretation. There's always room for new perspectives. Once a film is completed, it doesn't change (unless it's one of George Lucas's *Star Wars* films), but viewers—even when a film is first screened—vary widely, and the values a culture holds change over time. This is why submerged symptomatic meanings can have a tendency to surface as the years wear on. Sometimes, for later viewers, that's virtually all they can see when they watch one of these older films. Stepin Fetchit films are not as funny as they used to be.

Now let's look at a pair of climaxes. At the end of Disney's *Beauty and the Beast* (Gary Trousdale and Kirk Wise, 1991) the Beast magically returns to his human form (**1.15–1.17**).

We can compare this sequence to another climax. In *Shrek* (Andrew Adamson and Vicky Jenson, 2001) viewers are led to believe that Princess Fiona is about to return to her "true" human form (**1.18–1.20**).

Let's compare these sequences:

- In *Beauty and the Beast* Belle is taught to love the kind of beauty that's on the inside, and, for learning this lesson, she is rewarded with a prince who's beautiful on the outside. The film seems to be affirming the very same superficial value system it claims to criticize. Symptomatic meaning directly undermines the explicit message.

- The *Shrek* climax self-consciously "quotes" the Disney film, acknowledging the power of pyrotechnic effects and spectacle to render appealing virtually any story, no matter how troubling

1.15 *Beauty and the Beast.* The Beast's transformation is under way.

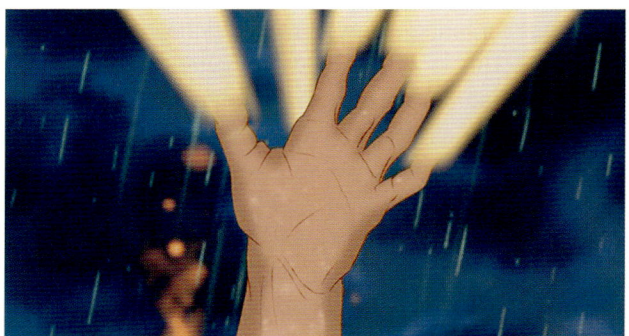

1.16 Light shoots from his fingertips.

1.17 The transformation is complete.

1.18 *Shrek*. Fiona's transformation is under way.

1.19 Light shoots from her fingertips.

1.20 The "transformation" is complete.

its underlying messages might be. Whereas in *Beauty* we have "magical" special effects crowned by a fireworks display, *Shrek* showily tops every one of these effects in an aggressively hyperbolic fashion.

- In *Shrek,* when the two ogres kiss, someone holds up an "Awwww" sign, and the crowd in the church complies by making this appreciative sound, as though the film, winking at us, is signaling that it knows what we want—and wants us to know it knows.

- After Fiona's fiery nontransformation, a stained-glass window remains unbroken. This the Dragon character punches out with her fist, indicating the film's wry willingness to accommodate any wishes that may linger for still more dazzle and noise.

- Then Donkey says, "I hoped this would be a happy ending," signaling yet again the film's awareness of audience expectations, and of the conventions the film simultaneously is invoking and subverting—for Fiona does not become a beautiful princess. The film seems to be conveying a message very different from the one implied in the Disney film. We might articulate it this way: *Love someone for who they are and maybe, just maybe, you'll be lucky enough to have them love you in return.*

An engagement with dominant cultural values that is this explicit can be viewed more as an *ideology critique* than as a symptomatic expression of the same. Yet there's always room for disagreement and further exploration. One might counter my progressive take on *Shrek* by pointing out that in this film, too, like kind ends up with like kind. The films are similar in that both imply that a happy ending will be one in which no romantic couplings cross any racial boundaries. But then one would have to account for *Shrek*'s outrageously unlikely coupling of the Donkey and Dragon characters.

One last text before we move on from symptomatic meaning: a magazine ad for a television called the Ambilight (**1.21**).

1.21 Advertisement for the Ambilight TV.

Let's consider this ad:

- It tells a simple story, with a "before" scenario on the left side and an "after" one on the right. The referential meaning of this ad can be summed up as follows: *a couple buys an Ambilight, and this increases their enjoyment of television.*

- The ad's explicit message can be stated even more succinctly: *you should buy an Ambilight TV.*

- In the "before" part, without the Ambilight enhancement, the woman isn't paying attention to the game. What is she paying attention to? Is she reading the *Wall Street Journal* or the *American Journal of Neuroscience?* No, she's looking at her nails. *After all, she's a woman.*

- The man, meanwhile, who didn't need the bells and whistles of the

Ambilight to follow the game, is even more involved after the switch. And look at the woman: now *even she* is watching the game.

- Finally, look at the lighting in the "after" part of the story and at the woman's uncomfortable, twisting frontality. Light and shadow model her breasts, making them appear more three dimensional, while her unnatural posture and orientation "offer" them to us, enticing us to believe that *everything* will be better after we buy this TV.

Any close look you take at a film can lead you to symptomatic meanings. There you may find expressions of cultural attitudes concerning race, gender, sexuality, class, and any number of other subjects.

EVALUATING FILMS: WHY NOT TO

There is a common approach to film analysis that, if you resist it, will improve the quality of your insights and the substance of your arguments. This is *evaluation,* which is saying whether you think a film is good or bad. This kind of commentary has its place in certain types of film writing, but when one is doing formal analysis, there are advantages to holding evaluation to a minimum.

For many coming to serious film study for the first time, the only model they have for talking about films is what reviewers do. Thumbs up. Thumbs down. 77 percent on the Tomatometer. The film is fast paced. It has expert editing. It has a weak third act. It's a masterpiece.

We all like and dislike things about the films we watch. The cinema is a sumptuous sensory feast. We can't help but react to films strongly, and we wouldn't wish it otherwise, for this is one of the great pleasures of watching movies. And these feelings can serve as great starting places for looking at a film more intently. But analysis differs from evaluation, and when one is looking at a film as a system of relationships and trying to develop persuasive arguments about what this system is doing, then evaluation, when it is more than a starting place, can really get in the way.

A place to be especially careful about evaluation is in thesis statements, which is where you articulate, typically at the end of your introduction, your essay's main claim. Also watch out for evaluation creeping in, and taking over, in conclusions. In these places, as elsewhere in your essay, to say a film is brilliant or a failure is to miss the chance to tell your reader something concrete and interesting about your film. If you fully commit to your ideas and work your arguments out carefully, your opinion of the film, positive or negative, will come across without your needing to spell it out.

When setting down your initial thoughts on a film, you might find yourself using evaluative language. *(That scene was awesome. Why is this character so annoying?)* This is natural and probably helpful as you sort through your notes and decide what you want to focus on. But clear away as much of that language as you can as you revise toward your final draft.

Making opinionated claims in a heated discussion with friends over pizza after seeing a movie is fine. It's better than fine; it's what many of us love to do. But when the goal is to craft a convincing argument that's grounded in the concrete formal particulars of a film, one is better off leaving evaluation to the critics.

FIVE PRINCIPLES

I've so far suggested two things to avoid when analyzing a film, namely, "content" and evaluation. A third is doing exclusively *thematic analysis,* as we've seen that themes are only one way to talk about film meaning, and meaning is part of the larger discussion of form. One last thing to go, but first, if we're not doing these things, what are we doing? What should we notice and look for when watching a film?

This chapter, up to now, has given some idea of an answer to this question, but we can get more specific. Bordwell and Thompson describe five principles of film form. These principles can guide your thinking as you watch a film and as you look at your notes afterward:

1.22 *The Quiet American.* Something a character reads . . .

- Function
- Similarity and Repetition
- Difference and Variation
- Development
- Unity/Disunity

Remember these principles, but as you watch, feel free to jot down *anything* that comes to mind. Don't edit or second-guess yourself while you're watching a film or thinking it over afterward. You'll winnow your argument down as you move toward your final draft, but early on, feel that anything goes and that more is better. You never know what might spark an epiphany or turn your thinking in an exciting direction later on.

Think of these principles as tools that can help you say what you want to say and, more important, help you *figure out* what you want to say. These tools are basic but powerful.

Function

Elements in films perform functions, often several at once. An element's function doesn't depend just on the film but on what you see in it. Very often, asking questions about function will lead you to ideas about themes

1.23 . . . triggers a memory (and a flashback).

and other sorts of messages a film might seem to be conveying. But remember that films are doing things besides suggesting meanings. Films that tell stories are channeling a lot of energy into that process, and your essay might look at how a film solves a narrative problem— arranges for a surprise, for example. If a film's hero and mysterious villain turn out to be, the climax reveals, one and the same person, the film's makers will need to have made a number of careful choices about how to organize the preceding hundred minutes of material. These problems might interest you, and you might be the first person to figure out how they were solved or even to articulate that they were problems in the first place. Chances are, moreover, that this sort of inquiry will bring you into contact with ideas about meaning whether you initially intended it to or not. In any case, when you approach a film and decide what about it interests you, keep an open mind as you think about the functions of the elements you are observing.

A concrete way to analyze function is to consider **motivation,** which is the *justification* for an element in a film being there. In *The Quiet American* (Phillip Noyce, GER/US/UK/AUS/FR, 2002) a character reads something that triggers a memory (**1.22–1.23**). This *flashback* (a term discussed in chapter 2) is motivated by the text this character reads. In *Down with Love* (Peyton Reed, 2003), when a character answers the telephone, the camera moves back as she walks into the foreground

1.24 *Down with Love.* The phone (bottom left) rings.

1.25 As the character comes forward to answer it, the camera backs up.

(**1.24–1.25**). What motivates this camera movement? The character movement does. As she comes forward, it seems natural—that is, justified—for the camera to back up and keep her in the frame. Because we can speak about most any element in a film in terms of its motivation, this term allows us to sift through the smallest textual details and ask precise questions about them.

Motivation might seem like a more straightforward concept than it is. Consider this moment in *Waltz with Bashir* (Ari Folman, Israel and other countries, 2008), when, during a street scene, a low glaring sun turns figures into silhouettes (**1.26**). What motivates this lighting? The sun does—but it doesn't cause the lighting. Motivation does not

1.26 *Waltz with Bashir.* The sun motivates stark lighting in this street scene.

mean "cause." There is no sun. This is a drawing in an animated film. But the sun justifies the lighting looking the way it does—just as, in a live-action film, a chandelier might motivate the lighting we see, even though most of this light is being produced by studio lights hung outside the frame.

What the author wanted. Function is one way to understand what a film's elements are doing. Another is to construe the elements as expressions of the film's "author," by which people usually mean its director. Before moving on from function, let's briefly consider this author-centered approach to films.

In a scene in *Cape Fear* (Martin Scorsese, 1991) the image switches from color (**1.27**) to black and white to a negative image (**1.28**) and then back again. When I show my students this sequence, they invariably have interesting things to say about it, including what these unusual choices might mean. The reason I show it is that I once attended an event at which Martin Scorsese took questions from the audience, and someone asked him why he did this in this scene. His response took several minutes, and long before he'd finished, it had become clear, at least to me, that he had no idea why he did this. He just thought it was cool.

Directors are not obliged to have a reason for every choice they make.

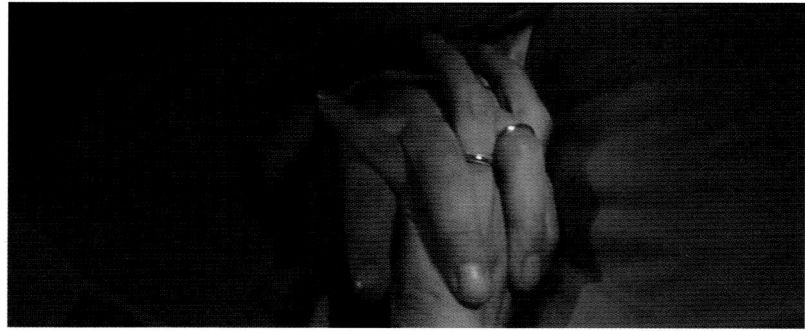

1.27 *Cape Fear.* The image . . .

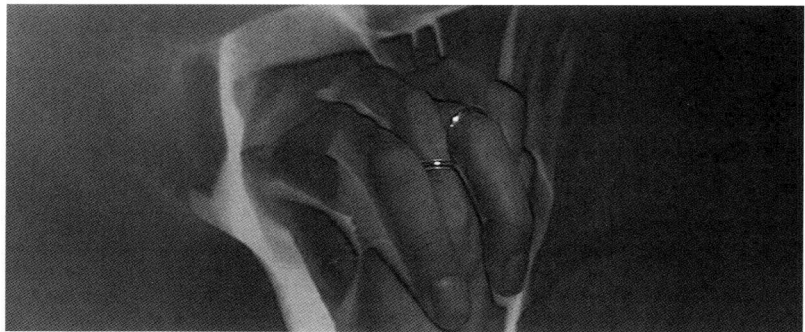

1.28 . . . switches to negative.

They can work as intuitively or as intellectually as they please and as the mysteries of the creative process allow. But if you are analyzing a film, then just because a director isn't sure why he did something doesn't mean that you can't have articulate and insightful things to say about the choices he made. Far from it.

We are not bound by considerations of author intention, and students doing formal analysis needn't trouble themselves with questions about it. In fact, they are generally better off if they don't. Making statements of author intention is the fourth and final thing I suggest you minimize or avoid altogether when writing about a film.

This comes down to refraining from saying things like "In this scene

Bigelow wants us to notice . . ." or "Hitchcock clearly did his homework on psychoanalytic theories of adolescence," or "Zhang's use of color shows his displeasure at the thought of . . ." You can still talk about how a film encourages us to notice something, resonates with this or that theory, or uses color to encourage viewers to feel a certain way —but look at the changes I made to the wording of these claims. The point is this: even if you're taking a course on, say, the films of Akira Kurosawa, in general, ask not *What is the director doing?* but *What is the film doing?*

This might seem like just a semantic difference, and in a way it is. But we can't get inside someone's head, even if the director said in an interview, "This is why I did such and such in my film." Maybe she's lying or doesn't remember her original reasons, or *maybe she's simply less interesting than her film is.* When researching a film, it can be fascinating and worthwhile to look at statements that have been made by its director, screenwriter, and other creative contributors. But treat these statements not as magic keys for unlocking the film but just as more texts to probe for possible meanings, including symptomatic ones, and to hold against other texts, including your film.

Ask not about *author intentions* but about *textual functions and effects.* The text, the film, is something you have in front of you. It's something you can speak about with authority because you can study and get to know it. You can analyze the elements in a film in terms of the functions they are performing.

Similarity and Repetition

Another formal principle you can observe operating in an artwork is *similarity and repetition.* Similarities and repetitions constitute patterns that bear in all sorts of ways on the film-viewing experience. Under this principle are two key terms: *parallelism* and *motif.*

Parallelism is when a film invites us to compare two elements by drawing our attention to similarities between them. The basis of the parallel can be anything, a line of dialogue or camera movement, for example.

1.29 "Kit for Cat" (Friz Freleng, 1948). First one visitor, . . .

1.30 . . . then another.

An instance of parallelism is the pair of almost identical shots of the bartender in *Groundhog Day* (**1.11–1.12**). Another is when, in a Looney Tunes cartoon, two cats bang on a door (**1.29–1.30**). A third is when, in an episode of *The Sopranos,* two characters unwind after a long day (**1.31–1.32**). Here are two forms of vice and indulgence. That the scenes come one after the other strengthens our sense of the similarity.

Another form of similarity and repetition is a **motif,** which is a recurring element in a film that we understand to hold some significance. As with parallelism, a motif can be anything—a camera angle, a color, a handkerchief. A motif developed in *Groundhog Day* involves a series of references to the weather. In *Secrets of a Soul* (G. W. Pabst, GER, 1926) a character with a pathological fear of knives encounters them every-

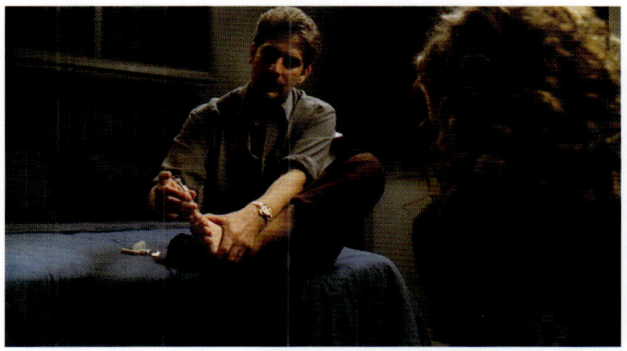

1.31 "For All Debts Public and Private," *The Sopranos,* seas. 4, ep. 1 (Allen Coulter, 2002). A character shoots heroin.

1.32 Another makes himself an ice cream sundae and watches TV.

where (**1.33–1.35**). Or a motif can be more abstract. Imagine that in the first scene of a film a character loses her car keys. You notice that throughout the film, characters keep slipping out of the frame, even though the camera is moving in an apparent attempt to keep them onscreen. You decide the frame keeps "losing" the characters. At the climax, a character loses his mind. You identify a motif that you call "losing things."

On the importance of motifs. The concept of the motif is a major one for us. Here's a way to think about why. Suppose you're writing a

1.33 *Secrets of a Soul.* In this self-consciously Freudian film, . . .

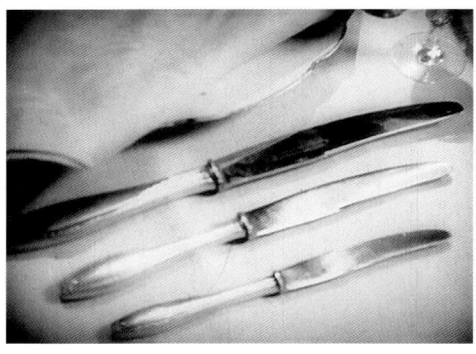

1.34 . . . knives and other sharp objects . . .

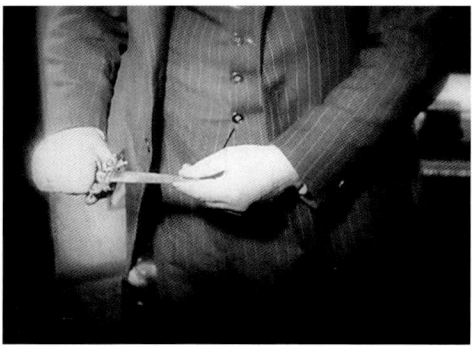

1.35 . . . provide clues to a neurotic character's problem.

paper, and you're noticing camera angles and editing patterns. These are technical things that might incline your reader, or yourself, to ask, "Who cares about this stuff?" But suppose you want to talk about bigger things—meaning, for example. You have opinions about what the film means, but it's just a feeling in your gut. You have no "proof," or, if you do, it's sketchy and vague. Now someone might say, in response to your claims, "That's just your opinion. Why should I believe you?"

The motif exists between these two levels of generality—between the surface texture of the film, with all its crowded minutiae, and the lofty heights at which we ask the Big Questions. And a motif points in both directions—up and down—and you can think of it as a sort of "transfer station" between these two levels. You're noticing these techniques but you don't know what, if anything, to make of them. See if you can organize them into patterns you can identify as motifs. If you can, you've moved in the direction of more abstract thinking, toward themes and other kinds of meaning—and you've done so in a way that will allow you to ground your claims in the concrete formal particulars of the film.

The same goes for parallelism, as well as for gaps, contradictions, and anything else you might find when you ask questions about motivation. I can't stress enough how important these principles are, how greatly they can transform the way you think about and watch films. And within this set of tools the motif is especially powerful.

Difference and Variation

Similarities prime us to notice differences. Comparing the expressions on the bartender's face (**1.11–1.12**) in *Groundhog Day* suggests to me that he's a little more impressed with Phil's pickup line than with Larry's. In the Looney Tunes cartoon (**1.29–1.30**), similarities in the two moments throw into relief how much smaller the second cat is than the first. And we note in *The Sopranos* (**1.31–1.32**) how much more culturally sanctioned and widespread the second character's indulgence is than the first's. The flip side of similarity and repetition is *difference and variation*.

Development

Development refers to patterned change across a film, any kind of progression. In the case of a story film many developments you'll observe will have to do with the narrative (discussed in chapter 2), but it's possible to spot developments in story films in other ways as well. The opening scenes in *Henry V* (Laurence Olivier, UK, 1944) resemble a stage production of Shakespeare's play, complete with a curtain, proscenium arch, and shots of the actors bustling about backstage. Then the look of the film changes, and flattish, brightly colored, painterly compositions call to mind the pages of a medieval illuminated manuscript. Then, for its climactic battle sequences, the film widens its scope and draws on conventions of the historical epic film genre, after which it reverts through these stages until we're back inside the theater in time for the actors' curtain call. This is a development we can trace across this film. It's possible, as well, to discern patterns of development in nonnarrative films such as experimental films.

Unity/Disunity

I began this chapter by referring to the ending of *The Sixth Sense,* when a major revelation makes everything that came before shift into a new and vivid configuration. One might come away from such a film praising its "tightness," saying it has no "plot holes." No element lacks motivation, and many are motivated in multiple ways. Such a film exhibits a pronounced degree of *unity.* Unity isn't necessarily a good or bad thing but just something, as with all of these principles, to notice and ask questions about.

A film that exhibits marked *disunity* might be one in which a character dies in the first third and reappears in the last third unharmed, with no explanation given. In the horror film *Vampyr* (Carl Th. Dreyer, GER/FR, 1932) a light appears in a darkened room, shining up from below (**1.36–1.37**). No source, physical or ghostly, is shown or otherwise attributed to this light. The lighting lacks motivation and introduces some disunity

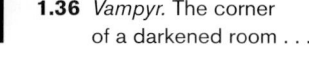

1.36 *Vampyr.* The corner
of a darkened room . . .

1.37 . . . begins to glow
inexplicably.

into the film. And yet, to the extent that we expect eerie things to happen
in a horror movie, this lighting can be said to be motivated (weakly) by
conventions of the film's genre.

Other instances of disunity are harder to account for. Near the end of
L'eclisse (aka *Eclipse,* Michelangelo Antonioni, IT/FR, 1962), two passionate lovers agree to meet later. The film then shows a nurse pushing
a baby carriage, a construction site, a streetlight flickering on, and other
images, many of which we've seen at earlier points in the film. Why does
it do this? Why does the camera tilt down from a high place and pause
on a deserted intersection? Viewers watch this wordless sequence and
wait for the lovers to show up, but the film refuses to deliver. We never
see them again. Where did they go?

This ending does display some unity, through its repetition of images we've seen before, and because it exhibits development—for over its course the day gradually darkens into night. But what this ending most strikingly delivers is a sizable hole in the narrative we've been following. We might be inclined to peer through this hole and look for a nonnarrative basis for the open ending, possibly a thematic one. Or maybe we're just left with questions. Challenging films like this one can inspire fruitful inquiries and investigations, just as more unified Hollywood films will offer equally rich opportunities for analysis and interpretation.

Even the most mainstream film will exhibit some disunity. One reason is that unity and disunity are, like so much else discussed in this chapter, partially matters of perception. When one is taking a viewer-centered approach to film, unity is in the eye of the beholder as much as it's a property of the filmic text. Further, unity isn't something black and white but rather exists on a scale of gradations.

A little prying and sifting will often reveal that some question was never answered or some dilemma remains unresolved. In *Groundhog Day,* for example, all the good deeds Phil commits as he journeys toward enlightenment are ostensibly for others, yet with each new dawn all his works are erased. The crisis of existential pointlessness the character faces in the dark middle stretch of the film is arguably one he never surmounts. Even as he grows and improves as a person, there remains something selfish about his actions: he's the only person who will ever remember them, the only one for whom they will hold any lasting value. For all his good deeds, nothing matters. Does the ending, when the spell is broken, undermine this pessimistic view of the film? This question, like so many of film interpretation, remains open to discussion and debate.

NARRATIVE

Now we move deeper into the specifics of film form. I have introduced the idea of thinking about films as systems. For films that tell stories, this system consists of two parts: *narrative* and *style*. These subsystems are so completely intertwined that they're inseparable, and though the interrelatedness of all the elements that make up a film is an ongoing emphasis of this book, we'll take these subsystems one at a time. Here in part 2 we consider film narrative. In part 3 we will turn to film style.

Film Narrative

Many if not most of the films we watch tell stories. A film's narrative con-stitutes a major subsystem within the total work. In this chapter we'll first consider some *narrative basics,* then turn to a vital force animating every film narrative, its *narration.*

NARRATIVE BASICS

What is a narrative? Most simply, a **narrative** is a set of events unfold-ing in time and space, linked by cause and effect. We will come back to this definition, but first let's consider two sets of terms.

Plots and Stories

Two words that are often used interchangeably but mean different things are *plot* and *story.* A film's **story** includes everything that happens in the narrative, both events that are shown and ones viewers only infer. A scene takes place in a lawyer's office. Behind his desk is his law school diploma. An event in the story is that this lawyer graduated from law school, even though this is never depicted in the film.

A film's **plot** has a more literal and concrete nature than its story. It's all the events that are presented to viewers in the order in which they are presented. In the above scenario the law school graduation isn't part of the plot. But now suppose our film contains a scene in which we see the lawyer receive his diploma. And imagine the film shows us this scene at the end, in a flashback (a term discussed later in this chapter), after we have watched all his long years practicing law. Now the graduation is part of the plot, and where it falls is at its end.

When we think about these two terms, it might seem that the story comes first, and if we're looking at a film from a production standpoint —a film, say, that's been adapted from a short story—it does. But in a viewer-centered approach, we start with the film, what's on the screen. We start, that is, with the plot. Viewers watch the film and, from this, they piece the story together.

Diegetic and Nondiegetic Elements

Another term refers to the world in which a story unfolds. We call this world the **diegesis,** and from this noun we get two adjectives that are even more useful. When we say a film element is part of the story world, or diegesis, we say it's a **diegetic** element. In the bar at Mos Eisley, in *Star Wars: Episode IV–A New Hope,* a band of alien creatures plays a tune. People in the bar can hear this music because it's part of their world. It is diegetic music. Later in the scene, Han Solo kills a bounty hunter with his blaster. The gun, bounty hunter, and Solo's vest are all diegetic elements in the film.

Something in a film can be a **nondiegetic** element. Spaceships don't have to take evasive action to avoid hitting the upward crawl of yellow text that opens *A New Hope* because, even though this text appears to stretch back into the reaches of space, it is not *in* this space. The text is nondiegetic.

Deciding whether an element is diegetic or nondiegetic is usually a straightforward matter, but a film can challenge and even undermine this distinction. For example, an episode of *The Twilight Zone* reveals the source of an apparently disembodied narrating voice to be a man sitting in the same location as the characters (**2.1–2.3**). Something to keep in mind throughout this book is that a film element or moment that seems to straddle usually separate categories, or combine them, or create its own category can be an especially productive one to examine. Grappling with what term best applies and how best to apply it, when our

2.1. "Nick of Time," *The Twilight Zone,* seas. 2, ep. 7 (Richard L. Bare, 1960). A couple in a diner asks a question of the fortune-telling napkin holder at their table.

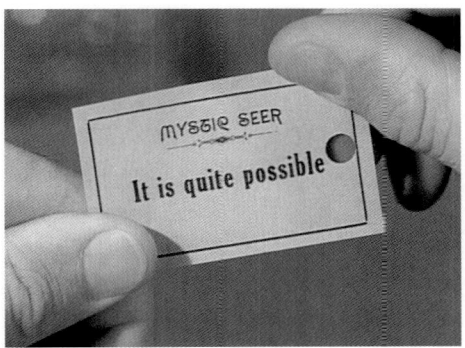

2.2. The voice of the show's host, Rod Serling, is heard saying, "The hand belongs to Mr. Don S. Carter, male member of a honeymoon team en route across the Ohio countryside to New York City." This voice seems to be coming from outside the story world.

2.3. But then the camera whips to another spot in the diner, and we see Serling talking directly to us. This is, after all, the Twilight Zone, where distinctions between things like waking and dreaming, reality and imagination, and diegetic and nondiegetic elements can become blurred.

terminology seems to break down or to be inadequate, can lead to unexpected insights into what is distinctive and interesting about a particular film.

Let's return to our definition of narrative. Out of it we can pull three concepts: *causality, time,* and *space.* We'll take these concepts one at a time.

Causality

Causality is the state by which events in a film exist in a relationship defined by cause and effect. Think of causality as the *glue* that holds a story film together. Consider this idea for a film:

A man gets out of bed and eats an English muffin. Then a dish falls off the kitchen shelf. His phone rings once and stops; the man doesn't answer it or even seem to notice. He watches some TV, scratches himself, and takes a shower. The end.

If it's hard to construe this set of events as a story, this is in part because these events are not linked by cause and effect. Without causality, all you have is a bunch of things happening.

Some films set events into cause-and-effect relationships more forcefully than others. One needn't say a film that does this is better than one that doesn't. They simply occupy different points along a continuum of possibilities available to filmmakers. Let's consider some of these possibilities.

In a film in which causality vigorously shapes how the narrative hangs together, we'll find Event A triggering Event B, which constitutes a new cause that triggers Event C, and so on. Near the end of *The Wizard of Oz* (Victor Fleming, 1939), Toto jumps out of Professor Marvel's balloon (cause), which prompts Dorothy to exit the balloon and go after her dog (an effect and a new cause), which results in her missing her ride back to Kansas (an effect and a new cause), and so on. A unified film can diverge from this sort of straight-line progression as well. Something that happens early on might not become important until later. In *M* (Fritz Lang, GER, 1931) a blind street vendor overhears a serial murderer whistling a tune as he approaches his next victim. Much later, the vendor hears the whistling again, setting off a manhunt that leads to the murderer's capture. Or a cause that occurs earlier in a *story* might be presented later in the *plot. Bullhead* (Michaël R. Roskam, Belgium/Netherlands, 2011) shows us a man who is dependent on a regimen of drugs. We won't know why until a flashback reveals the horrific childhood event that made the drugs necessary.

Showing an effect before revealing its cause is an order of presentation familiar from mystery films. In the mystery *The Maltese Falcon* (John Huston, 1941), private investigator Sam Spade's partner is murdered at the film's beginning, and only at the end is it revealed that Spade's client and love interest, Brigid O'Shaughnessy, killed him. Or a film might set two narrative lines into motion and make viewers wait to find out how the lines are, or will become, interrelated. *Deadfall* (Stefan Ruzowitzky, 2012) opens with a pair of casino robbers fleeing in their getaway car, then shows a former boxer being released from prison. These parallel developments won't knit together until more of the story has unfolded.

In a less unified film a major cause or effect might never be revealed. *Three Days of the Condor* (Sydney Pollack, 1975) ends with the main character telling a CIA director that he's gone to a newspaper with his story of murderous skullduggery in that organization, thus saving himself from almost certain death at the CIA's hands. The director asks, "How do you know they'll print it?" The protagonist looks momentarily stricken, then replies, "They'll print it." But the film ends by freezing on his image as, just before melting into the crowd, he looks back nervously over his shoulder. We never learn if the paper ran his story. In other films the disunity isn't momentary but infiltrates the work's overall composition. *L'eclisse* (discussed in chapter 1) exhibits a slackened and opaque causality throughout, conveying the characters' sense of drift and ennui as they fail to make meaningful connections with each other (**2.4**).

The "causes" in films tend to be **characters,** and it's primarily through the characters that the effects tend to reverberate. In other words, we watch the characters to see what they do and to see what happens to

2.4 *L'eclisse*. When the lovers embrace, the woman's expression is hard to read. Is she troubled by something? What? The film to this point has provided no clear answer. She and the man will make plans to meet, but, the film suggests, they never do. Is the film here showing us a sign of the doubt that will lead to their affair's unraveling? We can only guess. The causal connections, like the woman's emotions at this moment, are unclear.

them and the other characters as a result of their actions. These characters possess attributes, which, in a mainstream film, tend to be established boldly at the outset. Characters are often conventional types (the young girl is headstrong and impetuous; the old man is kindly and wise). Another convention (see chapter 1 on this term) is for a main character to change over the course of the story. Often he or she learns something. Scarlett O'Hara, in *Gone with the Wind* (Victor Fleming, 1939), learns that her true love is not, after all, the weak Ashley Wilkes but the dashing and good-hearted Rhett Butler, who has loved her all along. (The *outcome* of Scarlett's realization makes this film less conventional than other Hollywood films of its time and type.)

Cinematic Time

We extracted three terms from the definition of narrative. A second one is *time.* There are many ways a film can manipulate time as it builds its own **temporality** or "time-sense." Three variables filmmakers work with are the *order* in which the events are presented, their *duration,* and their *frequency.*

Order, duration, and frequency. A plot may show events in an **order** that differs from their chronological order in the story. The most common way is through a **flashback,** in which the film skips back to show an event that happens earlier in the story, then returns to where it left off and continues on. A film might present all or most of its action in a flashback, with brief scenes set in the present bracketing the flashback off. The film noir *Double Indemnity* (Billy Wilder, 1944) is a famous example. Or a film might interweave flashbacks more elaborately through the narrative and even embed one inside another. In *The Curious Case of Benjamin Button* (David Fincher, 2008) a woman reads in Benjamin's diary about a man describing a time he was struck by lightning. We see the woman reading (**2.5**), then the man telling the story (**2.6**), then the lightning strike (**2.7**). The film later returns us to the woman and the narrative's "present."

Different things can, recalling a term from chapter 1, motivate a flashback. In *Benjamin Button* the first flashback is motivated by a woman reading a diary, and the second one is motivated by a man telling a story. Or a film might present events out of order without such justifications. An example of a film that freely and boldly reorders chronological events is the crime-gone-wrong film *The Killing* (Stanley Kubrick, 1956).

Rarer is a **flashforward,** in which the plot shows us an event that takes place *later* in the story, then returns to the earlier point on the time line and continues. Unlike a flashback, a flashforward can't be motivated by a character's memory or by someone explaining to someone else what happened in the past. It therefore tends to seem like a deliberate reshuffling of the order of events, something imposed on the action from the outside rather than arising from it organically.

Filmmakers also work with temporal **duration.** It's rare for a film to structure its narrative in "real time," meaning that the time it takes for the story to transpire for the characters matches exactly how long it takes for it to unfold on the screen. A famous example is Alfred Hitchcock's

2.5 *The Curious Case of Benjamin Button.* A woman reads in a diary . . .

2.6 . . . about a man telling Benjamin about a time when he was struck by lightning. This is the first flashback.

2.7 Then we see the lightning strike, in a flashback nested inside a flashback.

Rope (1948), in which, all in one evening, two characters commit a murder and then host a dinner party that might or might not culminate with the discovery of their crime. Much more common are films that manipulate duration in various ways.

We can break duration into *story duration, plot duration,* and *screen duration.* **Story duration** is the timespan across which a story unfolds, whether or not all the events are explicitly depicted in the film. In our first lawyer's office example, the time the lawyer spent in law school is part of the story duration, even though we never see him attend or graduate. **Plot duration** is just the time that is represented. A plot's duration might center on a concentrated period—a tense night of hostage negotiations, say—or consist of bits and pieces of time spread over weeks, years, or centuries or more of story time. **Screen duration** is the run time of a film. A ninety-three-minute film has a screen duration of ninety-three minutes.

In the unusual case of *Rope,* story duration equals plot duration equals screen duration. In a more typical film, these will be made to differ from each other through various means. Two we'll learn about in chapter 4 are *fast* and *slow motion,* in which an action—a character running, say—takes up less or more screen time, respectively, than story time. An event can also be elongated or compressed through editing, as we'll see in chapter 5. Or, as happens at the end of *Three Days of the Condor,* a film might simply freeze the image, suspending story time while screen time ticks on.

How many times an event is represented is its **frequency.** In most films the frequency of each event equals one. That is, each event is represented one time. There are exceptions. Early in *Pulp Fiction,* two people eat in a diner. One shouts, "Garcon, coffee!" Moments later, the couple decides to rob the diner. The shout for the server means little to us the first time we hear it. The second time, late in the film, the line carries much greater weight because it brings us back to a precise moment and place in the story and tells us what's going to happen next, when we're watching two different characters whom we have come to care about greatly.

Another film that plays with frequency is *Run Lola Run* (Tom Tykwer, GER, 1998). Three times we watch the phone Lola tosses into the air clatter into its cradle. She's just received a call from her boyfriend, who is in desperate trouble with a gangster. Lola then begins a frantic run to save his life. The frequency of Lola hanging up the phone equals three. However, what makes this instance of repetition more complex is that each time Lola runs, her efforts yield different results. The film, which divides into three parts, shows us three possible futures for this character and her boyfriend. Does, then, the frequency of Lola hanging up equal three, or is each event, within its own parallel reality, unique? This inventive film challenges and warps our definitions and understandings of cinematic time and causality as most narrative films construct them.

Cinematic Space

Analogous to time, cinematic space breaks into *story space, plot space,* and *screen space.* **Story space** is the space wherein a film's story unfolds, whether or not it's explicitly depicted in the film. The school the man attended in our first lawyer's office example exists in story space, even though we never see it. **Plot space** consists just of the pieces of story space we're shown: an apartment and the alleyway outside; the roof of the Korean embassy; the bottom of the Marianas Trench. **Screen space** is what we can see in the frame at a given moment. Suppose the frame cuts a character off at the waist. You saw, a moment ago, that this character is sitting on a bicycle. Now, as you watch her from the waist up, the bicycle is in story and plot space but not in screen space.

As with time, our consideration of space will carry across the four chapters on film style.

NARRATION

Like motifs in the last chapter, a crucial concept in this one is *narration.* What is narration? The word might call to mind a film's narrator, the unseen speaker who sometimes escorts us into a plot's action: "It was a rainy night in 1947 . . ." This is part of what we mean by *narration,* but here we can compare the term to *motivation* in the last chapter. When many people consider motivation in relation to a film, they immediately think of the characters. Why do they do what they do? What goals impel them to act? To what are they reacting? Actors rehearsing a scene might ask their director, "What's my motivation?" But we learned that why the characters do what they do is only a small part of what motivation can refer to, that any element in a film can be viewed in terms of its motivation. Likewise, while that narrating voice would be part of a film's narration, the term encompasses much more. It can be applied in an analysis of virtually any aspect of a film, and this broad applicability helps to make narration a powerful concept.

Narration, because it's so central to narrative, relates in all sorts of ways to causality, time, and space. But what is it? **Narration** is the means by which a film parcels out story information, in the form of the plot, to shape the viewing experience in particular ways. If a narrative is a *thing,* an entity, a system, narration is more of a *process.* There's something dynamic and always changing about it. And the closer we move to a film's formal machinery—that is, the finer grained our analysis becomes —the more intricately we can see narration at work. In chapter 1 we considered how films can cause us to feel curiosity, suspense, and surprise. These are the sorts of effects that get orchestrated by a film's narration. There are many others, and the range of possibilities is as wide as the total creative spectrum that comprises the art and richness of the cinema.

Getting specific, we can envision narration varying along two axes. Bordwell and Thompson call these the *range of story information* and the *depth of story information.* What these two phrases mean might seem straightforward as you read about them, but they're easily confused with each other. My advice is to go slow, underline, and consider the following examples carefully.

Restricted versus Unrestricted Narration

First we'll consider the *range of story information*. When we look at a whole film, or at just a scene or moment in one, we can ask how *restricted* or *unrestricted* the narration is. This question comes down to how much a viewer knows in relation to how much the characters know. If we're following a particular character in a film or scene, we ask how much we know in relation to that character. We can clarify this by returning to the concepts of surprise and suspense.

Imagine a character in a scene doesn't know what's in the envelope on the kitchen table. Neither do we. He opens it, and we learn at the same moment he does that he's just inherited a fortune. Because we know only as much as the character does, this is **restricted narration.** We can note that restricted narration assists filmmakers in creating *surprise* and that it centrally structures the narratives of mystery films.

Now suppose we know what's in the envelope because, in the film's opening scene, we saw the dying uncle name this character in his will. Then we come to the scene at the kitchen table, and the character, despairing because he can't afford to pay for the operation that will save his wife's life, is getting ready to swallow a bottle of sleeping pills, which happens to be on the table next to the unopened letter. He picks up the letter, puts it down, picks up the bottle, goes to the sink and fills a glass with water, puts down the glass. This melodramatic film is toying with us. The narration has loaded us with information. We know the character might kill himself, and we also know, *unlike* him, that the answer to his prayers is in the envelope. And now the film is making us sweat while we wait to see what happens. Will he kill himself or open the letter? This kind of emotional engagement, we learned in chapter 1, is *suspense.* The sequence has elicited this response in part by giving us *more* information than the character possesses—that is, by making the narration **unrestricted.**

Unrestricted narration gives viewers more information than the characters. It can go so far as to appear **omniscient,** soaring off and showing us things that no character knows or perhaps ever will. A character wonders what another one is thinking at that very moment. Suddenly we're two thousand miles away and seeing this other character, who's writing in her journal about her mother. Or a toddler plays in a sandbox. The film cuts to the same character, fifty years later, perishing in a sandstorm, then returns from this flashforward to the sandbox. (Someone analyzing this sequence might, recalling a term from chapter 1, call this an instance of parallelism.) Narration that is this informed, and that displays its knowledge this flamboyantly, is omniscient narration.

For reasons that will become clearer below, picture the range of story information as a horizontal line (chart 2.1), with the left end marking the most restricted kind (we know no more than the characters) and the right end marking the most unrestricted kind (omniscient):

<table>
<tr><td>Most restricted</td><td>Most unrestricted</td></tr>
</table>

Chart 2.1   **RANGE OF STORY INFORMATION**

Objective versus Subjective Narration

The *depth of story information* refers to how *subjective* the narration is —across a whole film or just in a scene or at a given moment. How can narration be subjective? That is, how can a film bring us into the mind of a character? One way is through a technique that will come up again in chapter 5, the **point-of-view shot,** in which a film shows us a view of diegetic space that we construe to be from the physical vantage point of a character. A point-of-view shot can encourage us to identify more closely with a character by "putting us in his or her shoes." In *Umberto D.* (Vittorio De Sica, IT, 1952) a young woman looks out a high window and sees her lover below. We see the woman looking (**2.8**), then a point-of-view shot that shows us what she sees (**2.9**). She's excited to see him, and the film invites us to share her happiness by letting us share her perceptual point of view. Such a shot doesn't always increase character identification, however. We see through the night-vision goggles of the serial killer in *The Silence of the Lambs* (Jonathan Demme, 1991), but we identify with his trembling quarry, the character we see, more than with the psychopath whose vision we share. Still, in general, point-of-

2.8 *Umberto D*. The woman looks out the window.

2.9 A point-of-view shot shows her lover waving far below.

view shots increase the depth of story information, meaning they make the narration more subjective.

We can go deeper inside a character's mind. In *North by Northwest* (Alfred Hitchcock, 1959) a character who's been force-fed a bottle of bourbon tries to get away from his would-be killers. We see not only point-of-view shots from behind the wheel but also the road as the man, in his intoxicated state, sees it (**2.10–2.11**).

We can go deeper still. We might gain access to a character's thoughts. In *Written on the Wind* (Douglas Sirk, 1956) a woman remembers a conversation with her childhood sweetheart, and we hear them speaking (**2.12**). Flashbacks motivated by a character's memories (as in **1.22– 1.23**) are examples of narration deepening a film's subjectivity and therefore of increasing the depth of story information.

2.10 *North by Northwest.* The intoxicated driver . . .

2.11 . . . sees double.

2.12 *Written on the Wind.* As a character remembers happier times, we hear her voice as a young girl: "When we grow up, you'll marry me, won't you Mitch? I love you so much."

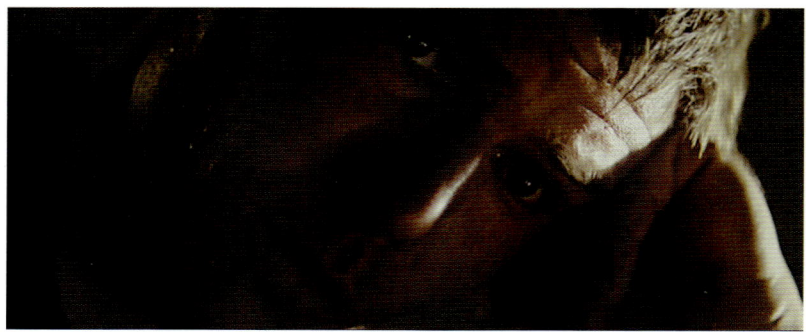

2.13 *Blade Runner: The Final Cut.* The character sees an image in his mind . . .

2.14 . . . and we see it on the screen.

Can narration be more subjective than when it's showing us, or letting us hear, a memory? Arguably, to grant us access to a private fantasy is to take us even deeper. In *Blade Runner: The Final Cut* (Ridley Scott, 1982/2007) a character imagines a unicorn (**2.13–2.14**). The film sets this subjective material clearly off as such; viewers aren't confused about where the unicorn is coming from. Other films are less forthright about what is and is not subjective. The German Expressionist film *The Cabinet of Dr. Caligari* (Robert Wiene, GER, 1920) reveals only at the end that the entire preceding action has been recounted by a highly unreliable narrator, a madman.

Recall the representation of the range of story information as a hori-

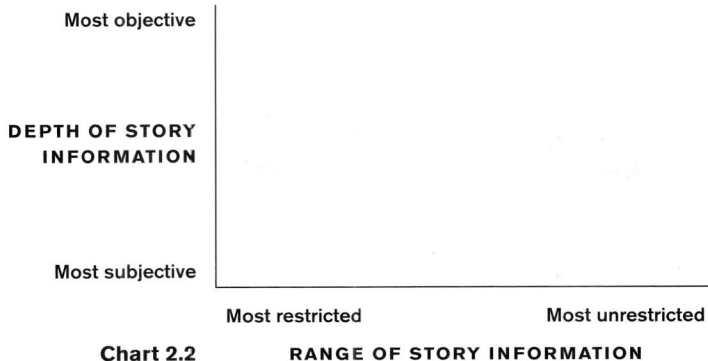

Most objective

**DEPTH OF STORY
INFORMATION**

Most subjective

Most restricted   Most unrestricted

Chart 2.2   **RANGE OF STORY INFORMATION**

zontal line. If we make the depth of story information a vertical line and set it at the range's left edge, we get chart 2.2.

Putting the Range and Depth of Story Information Together

As we think about how a film's narration can vary along these axes, two points bear emphasizing. First, return to the scene in which the character might open the letter on the table. In either of our two scenarios, *whether we don't know what's in the envelope (and so the range is restricted) or we do know (and so it's unrestricted), this sequence could include point-of-view shots.* This is because the range of story information and the depth of story information are two different things. This can cause confusion, because it might seem that a character whose subjectivity we share will be one whose knowledge (and no more) we also share— that is, that subjective narration and restricted narration are the same thing. But they're not. A film might feature dozens of point-of-view shots, and even sequences that show us a character's thoughts, but also tell us things this character only learns later or never learns. In other words, a film can combine subjective and *un*restricted narration. Or a film might include *no* point-of-view shots and also limit the narration to what a character knows. That is, a film can combine objective and restricted

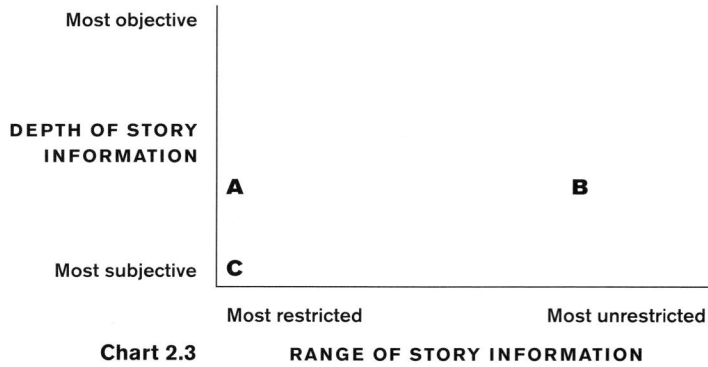

Chart 2.3   RANGE OF STORY INFORMATION

narration. The range and depth of story information are two different things.

Look at chart 2.2 again. Where on it would you locate the letter-on-the-table scene if viewers don't know what's in the envelope but the scene includes point-of-view shots? The scene would go somewhere around where I place the A on chart 2.3, because the narration is somewhat subjective and also restricted. Now picture a scenario in which we get the same point-of-view shots but we do know what's in the envelope. See the B, for narration that's just as subjective but now unrestricted. Last, in the "Final Cut" version of *Blade Runner,* we see, some time after the fantasy sequence, another unicorn that introduces the possibility that this character, whose job is to hunt down and kill "replicants" (robots that are hard to tell apart from humans), might be a replicant himself. Viewers who come to this conclusion (on the basis of evidence that, for some viewers, is far from conclusive) don't know this when they watch the fantasy sequence. Neither does the character. So, for narration that's deeply subjective and also restricted, see where I place a C.

Insightful analysis will rarely come down to points on a chart. Your written reflection on a film will be more interesting and imaginative than my schematic overview, but hopefully I've given you a sense of how these ideas can work together.

2.15 *Jeepers Creepers.* While we hear Jezelle say, "You hurt it, out there on the road, but only as much as it *can* be hurt," we watch the monster lurch toward the station.

Second, while a whole film, a whodunit mystery for example, might be characterized by one type of narration—tightly restricted with, say, moderate subjectivity—a great power of the concept lies in how we can use it to track choices and changes in a film from moment to moment. Films can take viewers on heart-pounding thrill rides and on journeys with the minutest turns and the tiniest atmospheric fluctuations, and some-times a single film will do all these things before the end credits roll. The regulating armature running underneath it all will be the film's narration.

NARRATION IN A SCENE FROM
JEEPERS CREEPERS

Let's conclude with an example of how a film's narration can change over the course of a scene. In the horror film *Jeepers Creepers* (Victor Salva, 2001) a brother and sister drive through a remote southern coun-tryside on their way home from college. Along the way they encounter a truck that nearly forces them off the road. Increasingly terrifying en-counters with the truck lead the siblings eventually to run the driver over repeatedly and speed off. They come to a police station and, in this scene, learn what they already suspected: this was no ordinary driver and not even "merely" a crazed killer. Viewers, too, have only slowly come to this realization, as up to this point, the narration has been restricted. As the mysterious driver became more aggressive, we wondered, along with the characters, what was going on and how bad things were going to get.

Now, at the police station, a character, Jezelle, who knows something about this creature, fills the brother and sister in. As we learn how fearsome and unstoppable this monster is, so do the siblings, and in this respect the narration stays restricted. But more is going on in the sequence, for intercut with Jezelle's explanation are shots that make viewers privy to information no one inside the station possesses. The creature, who didn't die when the siblings ran it down, has just pulled up outside and is on his way in (**2.15**). When, a moment later, all the lights in the station go out, we know more than the characters do, and this greatly increases our sense of suspense and dread while the rest of the scene plays out.

This sequence is notable for how, in the context of the larger film, it slides the narration from restricted to unrestricted at a moment calculated to ratchet up the tension and terror. By controlling how it parcels out story information, the film has elicited our strong emotional involvement.

STYLE

Story films break into narrative and style. Chapter 2 was about film narrative. The next four chapters are about **film style,** which is the sum of all the techniques that concretely make up a film. Now, as we move closer to the surface of the film, the terms of our analysis grow less abstract. A filmmaker decides to restrict the narration in a scene. That's pretty vague. How exactly does she do this? She needs to make decisions, like where to put the camera, when and whether to cut from one angle to another, and where to place the actors and how and whether they should move. These are the specific choices that together add up to the film we see on the screen. And filmmakers are constantly making choices. Move the actor closer to the camera or cut to a closer view? Show the dream sequence in color or black and white? Have the character just describe the phone conversation or show it in a flashback—and then, show only him talking or cut back and forth between the speakers? Filmmakers bring a powerful tool kit to every task. *And something is always gained or lost when one choice is favored over another.* The next four chapters, more than the ones before now, get into the specific tools in this kit. We'll divide style into four major components: *mise-en-scène, cinematography, editing,* and *sound.*

Two things before we get started. First, the pages that follow move briskly through a lot of techniques. As you're encountering the definitions and illustrations, remember that a value of knowing these terms and details is that you can organize the elements that make up a film into patterns and look for things like motifs, instances of parallelism, unity and the lack of it, and motivation and the lack of it; and you can, based on your observations, take a step toward still more abstract thinking and formulate ideas about film meaning. You can craft an essay argument that your reader will find insightful and convincing. You might not impress your friends when you point out that a particular shot in a film is a medium long shot, but you will know that this sort of detail can be shown to matter through careful analysis and that an analysis that lacks attention to such details can appear overly subjective and vague.

Second, before we get to the first component of film style, here is a term that we'll be calling the basic building block of cinema: the **shot,** which is a length of film that has no breaks in it. Everything in the chapters ahead relates in some way to this basic building block of cinema. The next two chapters—on mise-en-scène and cinematography—describe two ways of looking at the shot. Chapter 5 is about combining shots, that is, editing. Chapter 6 considers film sound and its relationship to the cinematic image.

Mise-en-scène

Originally a French theatrical term meaning "put in the scene," **mise-en-scène** is everything in front of the camera. If we imagine our basic building block, the shot, as a box, mise-en-scène is everything inside this box. Mise-en-scène splits into four main categories—and let me stress that starting now, we really begin to move systematically through a large set of terms. I'll continue to remind you where we are in the big picture—what umbrella term we're underneath and what term that term is underneath—but your efforts will pay off if you review these relationships as you go. The four categories of mise-en-scène are *setting, costume and makeup, lighting,* and *staging.*

Once a space is filmed, it is transformed in ways that we'll look at in this chapter. This space, before it's transformed, is called **profilmic space.** Think of profilmic space as the visual raw material a camera takes in and turns into mise-en-scène. The notion of profilmic space might seem increasingly quaint as, more and more in mainstream films, there may be no profilmic space at all, or less of it anyway, as filmmakers create new spaces and modify existing ones on computers. Still, thinking about profilmic space as something captured and transformed by the camera continues to be a useful way to think about film art, for as we look at this "stuff in the box," we'll be asking how the elements in front of the camera resolve into images on a flat screen. When we do, we'll be considering *composition* and asking questions of a sort that, if you've studied painting or photography, you may have asked before. Much of the art of cinema lies in this transformation from three dimensions into two.

STYLIZATION

One last idea to introduce before we move into the specifics of mise-en-scène is that an element in a film can be more or less *stylized*. This is a useful term because stylization is the other side of the coin of "realism," and it can be easier to describe how something is stylized than to describe how it is "realistic." (Realism might seem like a straightforward idea, but what people mean by it varies considerably.) **Stylization** pushes an element in a film outside the bounds to which we might expect the element, if we encountered it in daily experience (or perhaps another film), to conform. It's not, strictly speaking, how much the element differs from "reality" that is most important. In a viewer-centered approach, stylization is more a matter of perception than of objectively measuring a film element's deviation from the real thing. And yet while the standards of judgment will be subjective, most would agree that Fred Flintstone's prehistoric car is more stylized than the Batmobile (pick your version) and that the Batmobile is more stylized than a Toyota Prius.

Stylization is a matter of perception and also one of degree. Consider the Disney film *The Princess and the Frog* (Ron Clements and John Musker, 2009). How stylized is this film? Surely its characters and settings look more "cartoonish" than the ones seen in most live-action movies (**3.1**). But consider the moment when, in the scene pictured, a character bursts into song and the look of the film changes dramatically (**3.2**). The color scheme shifts to a brighter palette; finer details of face, costume, and setting vanish; and the figures seem to be less bounded by gravity and the limits of human anatomy than they did moments ago. If the film was stylized before, it has become more so with the start of this number. Stylization is a matter of degree.

SETTING

Our first component of mise-en-scène is **setting,** which is the physical environment wherein a film's action takes place. Broadly, we can speak of two pairs of options.

3.1 *The Princess and the Frog.* Tiana (right) and her mother visit the old sugar mill where Tiana hopes one day to open her own restaurant.

3.2 As she begins singing "Almost There," imagining herself running the restaurant, the film becomes more stylized. The art deco look of the number mirrors an illustration, torn from a magazine, on which her father wrote "Tiana's Place" years ago, when she was a little girl and he taught her to work hard for her dreams.

Location and Studio Filming

First, filmmakers can use an actual setting ("shot on location in the Florida Everglades") or build one—and, increasingly in mainstream film-making, building a setting can mean creating one, wholly or in part, digitally with computers. Using an existing locale can be associated with notions of realism—and also with low-budget filmmaking, since it's usually cheaper to shoot in, say, an actual diner than to build one. Or, if it's a hard-to-reach place, location shooting can be associated with *big-budget* filmmaking. During the Hollywood studio era (roughly 1917 to 1960), the increased costs of building sets versus going on location were often judged to be worth the corresponding gain in control. No need to worry about rain pelting the diner window and delaying shooting or ruining a take if the diner is inside a soundstage, and the rain will only fall if the filmmakers wish it. Today, computer-generated environments afford filmmakers greater control than ever before.

Parts of the Soviet Montage film (a movement discussed in chapter 5) *Storm over Asia* (aka *The Heir to Genghis Khan,* Vsevolod Pudovkin, USSR, 1928) were shot on the Mongolian plains. This historical fiction film shows, in documentary fashion, landscapes, indigenous dwellings, and rituals that remain fascinating today for the rare glimpses of remote locations, peoples, and cultural practices they provide (**3.3**). Location shooting contributes to impressions of this film's realism, while settings in *Frankenstein* (James Whale, 1931) practically flaunt their studio-built artificiality (**3.4**), a quality that some admirers of the film find contributes to its nightmarish atmosphere.

Stylized and Unstylized Settings

Second, a setting can be more or less stylized. That is, the degree to which it meets our expectations based on our sense of such a place in the real world, or perhaps another film, can vary. This might seem like a rewording of the "built versus found locale" distinction above, but in fact built sets can be rendered indistinguishable from found ones, and a found setting, filmed from certain angles and with certain lighting, can be made to appear strange and unreal. Examples of stylized settings are in *Careful* (Guy Maddin, Canada, 1992), a contemporary film with a deliberately antiquated look and sound (**3.5**).

3.3 *Storm over Asia.* Location shooting.

3.4 *Frankenstein.* Studio-built "exteriors."

3.5 *Careful.* A stylized setting.

3.6 *Killer of Sheep* (Charles Burnett, 1979). A woman checks her reflection in a pot lid, a prop in the film.

Props

A film's setting includes props. A **prop** is an object that serves some function within the narrative (**3.6**). The spinning top at the end of *Inception* (discussed in chapter 1) is a prop. The ring that Frodo bears in the *Lord of the Rings* movies is a prop. So is the diary the woman reads in *The Curious Case of Benjamin Button* (**2.5**). Recall from chapter 1 that anything can be a motif. This includes props. In *The Seventh Seal* (Ingmar Bergman, Sweden, 1957) a character plays chess at different points in the story with a figure representing Death. The chess set is a prop and a motif. So are the knives in *Secrets of a Soul* (**1.33–1.35**).

COSTUME AND MAKEUP

An unstylized Civil War Confederate soldier costume would match, as accurately as possible, the cut, stitching, buckles, fabric, color, and wear and tear of an actual uniform as far as can be determined from drawings, photographs, and other archival sources. Or suppose some aspect of the original uniform has not been copied in Civil War films very often; a costume that duplicates *this* original aspect might strike some viewers as stylized. (In ancient Rome a thumbs-down gesture from the emperor meant *Let the defeated gladiator live;* in every gladiator film it means the opposite.) Notions of realism are shaped, like everything else in a film, by conventions. Still, if stylization is to an extent subjective, most viewers would nevertheless agree that the formal attire worn by the title character in *Willy Wonka & the Chocolate Factory* (Mel Stuart, 1971) is more stylized than that worn by the title character in *Lincoln* (Steven Spielberg, 2012).

What if there exists no direct real-world reference for comparison? Can we still call a character's costume or makeup stylized or unstylized? Consider the costumes in the science fiction horror film *Alien* (Ridley Scott, 1979). The wrinkled jackets and greasy caps of the spaceship crew, like the lived-in look of the ship's interior—the coffee cups and general clutter—would strike many viewers as less stylized than the brightly colored costumes and interiors in the cartoonishly futuristic *Flash Gordon* (Mike Hodges, 1980).

Like the other aspects of mise-en-scène, a character's costume or makeup can pick up colors or other details that play into a motif, provide clues to a character's nature or psychology, and contribute in striking or subtle ways to a shot's composition. A costume can also act as a disguise that a viewer might or might not see through. In *All about Eve* (Joseph L. Mankiewicz, 1950) the title character waits every night outside a Broadway theater stage door in the hopes of meeting her idol, Margo Channing. One night she manages to get backstage, where she quickly demonstrates her eagerness to pick up what crumbs of wisdom she can from this grande dame of the stage and to help out in every way that's asked of her. At this first meeting Eve wears a buttoned-up trench coat and frumpy hat. This plain, diffident girl is the picture of abject humility and fan worship. But it's all an act, for Eve is actually a treacherous, ruthlessly ambitious aspiring actress. Over the course of the story Margo, her friends, and we will learn all about Eve. Or consider, conversely, how one could argue that Eve's costume at this first meeting *does* tell us about her, since it covers up nearly every part of her body (she's even wearing gloves). This character, her costume seems to be announcing, is about nothing if not concealment and camouflage.

LIGHTING

A shot's **lighting** can come from diegetic sources of illumination (the sun, candles, lamps) within the setting, nondiegetic ones located outside the frame, or a combination. Two ways we can speak about lighting are in terms of its *quality* and *direction*—but first, to consider lighting is to consider shadows. Here are two kinds.

Two Kinds of Shadow

An **attached shadow** is a shadow cast by something onto itself because it's not fully illuminated (**3.7**). The side of a planet that's facing away from the sun it orbits is in darkness; this is an attached shadow. Noses cast attached shadows on faces. This kind of shadow helps to make objects appear more three dimensional. A **cast shadow** results when something is placed between an object and a light source such that a shadow of that something—tree branches, a person—falls on the object (**3.8**). A film may use shadows for expressive purposes, suggesting a character's interior state or foreshadowing events. In *Kiss Me Deadly* (Robert Aldrich, 1955) a character accuses private investigator Mike Hammer of taking the law into his own hands, saying that anyone who does that "might as well be living in a jungle." This accusation plays into a motif that draws on the way Hammer prowls around his apartment when he suspects that someone is hiding in it; the curiously treelike column in this space; and, in his building lobby, vine-patterned wallpaper and crisscrossing shadows that make the lobby resemble a dark animal lair.

Lighting Quality and Direction

Lighting quality can be *hard* and even harsh, such as in sunlight at noon or under an interrogator's lamp (**3.9**). Shadows are sharp-edged under this intense sort of lighting. Or lighting can be more *diffuse* (**3.10**), softening shadows and decreasing *contrast*—which is the amount of

3.7 *The Graduate* (Mike Nichols, 1967). Attached shadows on Benjamin's face.

3.8 He takes a few steps, and now the cast shadows of window blinds fall across him. This character is about to begin an affair with an older married woman that will plunge him into self-loathing and shame. Here, in the hotel room, cast shadows suggest the surreptitious nature of the encounter and also that Benjamin has walked into a trap.

difference between an image's darkest and lightest tones. (We will consider contrast in chapter 4.)

The image from *The Scarlet Empress* (**3.10**) is also useful for talking about **lighting direction.** Can you see where the light is coming from in this image? A way to tell is by looking at the direction in which the shadow of the nose is falling and at how the cheek hollows are darkening. These tell us the light is coming from above and to the right. Less flattering is **bottom lighting** (or underlighting). Characteristically seen in

3.9 *High Noon* (Fred Zinnemann, 1952). In this shot of this figure, who's about to face a band of killers alone, harsh daylight sets him off starkly against the empty background.

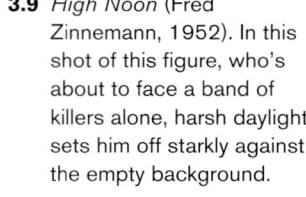

3.10 *The Scarlet Empress* (Josef von Sternberg, 1934). Diffuse lighting complements and accentuates the facial features of actress Marlene Dietrich.

horror films, this lighting comes from below and can cast grotesque shadows on faces and walls (**3.11**). Lighting from above is **top lighting** (**3.12**).

Sticking with direction, also evident in the *Scarlet Empress* image (**3.10**), is **backlighting,** which comes from behind. Backlighting commonly serves two purposes. First, it can make figures glow in a glamorous fashion, giving them a halo that renders them luminously unlike the ordinary people who populate the real world. Second, and especially important in black-and-white films, it helps separate figures from backgrounds, making them easier to pick out with the eye. Backlighting set to these purposes is sometimes called **edge lighting** (or rim lighting). When backlighting leaves figures entirely or predominantly in shadow, this is **silhouette lighting** (**3.13** and **1.26**).

3.11 *Dracula* (Tod Browning, 1931). A lamp seen in another shot motivates gruesome bottom lighting on the vampire as he closes in on his next victim.

3.12 *Shaft* (Gordon Parks, 1971). Top lighting on the title character as he stands in a phone booth.

3.13 *Osama* (Siddiq Barmak, Afghanistan/Ireland/JP, 2003). Silhouette lighting in a shot of demonstrators fleeing Taliban soldiers who have turned fire hoses on them.

Lighting in Classical Hollywood Cinema

The style of filmmaking that characterizes mainstream narrative films is **classical Hollywood cinema,** which has been around since the late 1910s and has since spread around the world. In this style backlighting combines with two other kinds in what is known as the **three-point lighting system.** A second of these lights is the **key light,** which is a shot's main lighting source, the one that, in *The Scarlet Empress* (**3.10**), comes from above and to the right. This light is usually motivated by a diegetic source, even if it's not the actual source of the lighting we see. (See chapter 1 on motivation.) Third is the **fill light,** which softens the shadows created by the key light and helps create a generally more flattering look for faces.

We can distinguish two major kinds of three-point setup. **High-key lighting** is relatively even, tends to be bright, and minimizes shadows (**3.14**). **Low-key lighting** provides little or no fill light, increases contrast, and results in darker and crisper shadows (**3.15**). Different genres are associated with each setup—comedies and musicals with high key; horror films, thrillers, and film noirs with low. But like the variations within these broad configurations, their possible applications are endless, and one must be cautious when making generalizations.

As with the other components of mise-en-scène, lighting can exhibit varying degrees of stylization. The shimmering lighting in the *Scarlet Empress* image (**3.10**) is an example of stylized lighting. The more extreme lighting in *Careful* (**3.5**) is another. The image from *Shaft* (**3.12**), a gritty urban crime drama, shows an example of unstylized lighting.

STAGING

Staging refers to what the figures in front of the camera do. We can think about staging in two ways: (1) acting and performance and (2) how the figures combine with other elements in the mise-en-scène to form patterns on the screen.

3.14 High-key lighting in the comedy *Monkey Business* (Howard Hawks, 1952).

3.15 Low-key lighting in *Blue Velvet* (David Lynch, 1986), a dark and disturbing thriller.

Acting and Performance

Unlike other aspects of film style, acting can be hard to analyze because we lack the terminology to describe exactly what, say, Marlon Brando is doing in the drama *On the Waterfront* (Elia Kazan, 1954) versus what Steve Martin is doing in the comedy *The Jerk* (Carl Reiner, 1979). Still, the concept of stylization can help. Martin engages in broad physical comedy, which no one expects to look real as long as it's funny. He grimaces, leaps around, balletically twists his body into ludicrous positions, and telegraphs his emotions in the most hyperbolic fashion. Brando, in contrast, keeps his gestures small and grounds everything he does in the psychology of his character. In this film's most famous scene, the washed-up boxer, feeling bitterly let down, and grieving over what might have been, pours his heart out to his brother, telling him, "I could've been a contender." The scene remains a benchmark, even a cliché, for great (that is, realistic) film acting. Whether or not one considers it great, Brando's performance is surely less stylized than Martin's.

Incisive close reading rests on a foundation of common sense, yet vivid, description of what is happening on the screen. Practicing this skill will serve you well as you consider the mercurial art of film performance in your formal analysis.

Shifting Patterns on the Screen

Staging also refers to the actors' positions and movements in front of the camera. Again, three dimensions resolve onto two, so moving figures will disappear behind other ones and behind objects in the setting and grow larger or smaller as they get closer to or farther from the camera. Staging is a delicate and underappreciated cinematic art. Tracing it as it unfolds from one moment to the next can lead you to discoveries of virtuoso orchestrations of figural movements and cinematic effects.

Figures can be arranged shallowly, strung laterally across the frame, or they can be set into the depth. When staging unfolds in a setting that has significant depth, and utilizes this depth, this is **deep-space staging.** We haven't covered editing yet, but in general, a film that relies less heavily on editing will rely more on staging to control its narrational flow and aesthetic appearance. Editing provides a means to guide viewers, but staging, whether or not a film minimizes editing, does this as well.

Figures can draw attention to themselves by moving or, conversely, by holding still in a shot in which other elements are in motion. Or the eye can be drawn to a figure when it turns to face us or when it comes closer to the camera so that it fills more of the frame. A figure turning its back to the camera can encourage us to look elsewhere, including at something we shouldn't miss—or we might become riveted to the rear-facing figure as we wonder what this person, whose face we can't see,

3.16 *Ugetsu* (Kenji Mizoguchi, JP, 1953). A desolate and abandoned woman staggers into a frame crowded with branches, posts, grass, and shadows. We easily pick her out as she steps first into one aperture frame . . .

3.17 . . . and then another.

3.18 In *Raise the Red Lantern* (Yimou Zhang, CH/HK/Taiwan, 1991) a household's servants and wives live within a rigid and oppressive social hierarchy. This geometric composition, one of many in the film (and so a motif), sorts the characters into their boxes, with the lowliest servants, further down the pecking order than the wives, occupying the compartments nearer the fringes.

3.19 *West Side Story.* Tony sneaks into Maria's bedroom.

is thinking. Another way to focus attention is through a device called **aperture framing,** in which windows, doors, and other enclosing shapes embedded in the mise-en-scène section off portions of the frame. Placing or moving a figure into one of these visual pockets will draw the eye to it, and the device can be set to other purposes as well (**3.16–3.18**). Last, staging can be more or less stylized. The image from *Careful* (**3.5**) provides a hint of the stiffly artificial staging in that film.

MISE-EN-SCÈNE IN A SCENE FROM *WEST SIDE STORY*

The four components of mise-en-scène can come together in rich and intricate ways. In *West Side Story* (Jerome Robbins and Robert Wise, 1961), a modern musical retelling of *Romeo and Juliet,* Tony is on the run after killing Maria's brother in a gang fight. He slips into Maria's bedroom through her window, and she, despite her shock and grief, lovingly welcomes him. In this scene they'll sing a duet titled "Somewhere."

A glass door (**3.19**) motivates expressive lighting later in the scene (**3.20**). Tony assures Maria, "We're really together now," but lighting splits the frame and portends otherwise for these star-crossed lovers (**3.21**). Seconds later, mise-en-scène separates them again as we view

3.20 The two embrace . . .

3.21 . . . . and sing "Somewhere." Lighting places them in separate zones within the frame.

3.22 Then a piece of furniture in the foreground does the same.

3.23 Then they stand, and a thick line on the wall behind them does it again. The more emphatically these two cling to each other and pledge their love, the more the film hints that they have no future together.

them through the ironwork footboard of Maria's bed (**3.22**). In the same shot, as they continue singing "There's a place for us . . . ," the two stand, and the scene sets a divider between them for a third time (**3.23**). There is no place for these two. One needn't know the outcome of Shakespeare's play to intuit that this young love is doomed.

Mise-en-scène, for all its complexity and power, is only one way to approach and analyze a shot. We consider a second way in the next chapter.

Cinematography

4

Story films divide into two subsystems, narrative and style, with style breaking into four components, the first two of which—mise-en-scène and cinematography—center on what we're calling the basic building block of cinema, the shot. With mise-en-scène we pictured the shot as a box—even though, of course, it isn't really a box. Mise-en-scène, as powerful a concept as it is, only gets us so far. Films are moving photography, and all sorts of things can happen over the course of a shot that never could if the contents of the frame really were in front of us as they are, say, on a theatrical stage. In this chapter we look at the shot in terms of **cinematography,** considering its *photographic nature,* a powerful aspect of cinema called *framing,* and a type of shot known as *the long take.*

Before we get started, it might help you pace yourself, and not feel discouraged if it seems there's a lot coming at you, if you know that this chapter introduces more techniques than any other in the book.

THE SHOT'S PHOTOGRAPHIC NATURE

Whether a cinematographer is shooting on traditional photochemical film or in a digital format, different qualities of the image owe to its photographic nature. Let's look at some of these qualities.

Tone, Texture, Color

A film image can have more or less **contrast** (first mentioned in chapter 3). A contrasty image contains strong blacks and whites with not much

4.1 *Ocean's Eleven* (Steven Soderbergh, 2001). In this color film a flashback is depicted in contrasty black and white.

4.2 *Man Bites Dog* (Rémy Belvaux, André Bonzel, Benoît Poelvoorde, Belgium, 1992). A less contrasty image.

in between (**4.1**). A less contrasty image contains fewer black blacks and white whites and shows more gradation in between (**4.2**).

Also like still photographers, filmmakers control **exposure,** which is how much light entering the lens is allowed to reach the photographic film or digital sensor inside the camera. An exposure can yield results that approximate what your eye would see if you were standing at the filming location, but a range of differences is also possible. In *End of Watch* (David Ayer, 2012) two police officers enter a crime scene (**4.3**). The shot is exposed for the house interior, and the result is to **over-expose** the portion of the frame seen through the doorway. It's brighter

4.3 *End of Watch.* The area of the frame around the center figure is overexposed.

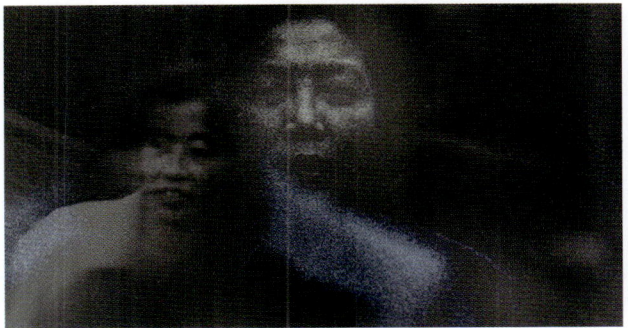

4.4 *The Fog of War: Eleven Lessons from the Life of Robert S. McNamara* (Errol Morris, 2003). A grainy composite image.

outside, and exposing for that part of the image would have required letting less light through the lens. Instead, the space seen through the doorway is washed out, adding to the overall documentary feel of the film. By contrast, to **underexpose** a shot is to let in too little light, unbalancing the image in the other direction and darkening it.

A third photographic quality is a potential by-product of the photochemical film process, sometimes desirable, and something that can be simulated in digital cinematography. This is *graininess*. A **grainy image** has a roughened visual texture. The particles of film emulsion that make it up are large enough to be noticeable (**4.4**). In a less grainy image these particles are smaller, and the image has a sharper appearance (see **4.1** for an example).

Last, alongside the choices available when thinking about mise-en-scène, filmmakers exercise a variety of options for controlling the color of the photographic image, from tinting and toning techniques dating back to the silent era (see **5.26–5.27** for examples), to lens filters that alter a shot's color (and exposure), to digital processes that are constantly evolving. **Digital color grading** in the *Lord of the Rings* movies, for example, gives different settings—the hobbit homeland of the Shire, the dwarves' Mines of Moria, and so on—their own range of hues. This process enhances color choices made in the design of the settings, costumes and makeup, and lighting, bringing out, for example, the warm greens and other earth tones of the Shire. Digital grading also helps computer-generated imagery (CGI) blend more smoothly with live-action elements, and it can be used to create lighting effects, spotlighting, for example, absent at the time of filming.

Fast and Slow Motion

Unlike still photographers, filmmakers can manipulate the speed of motion. Filming at a rate higher than the standard sound-film shooting rate of twenty-four frames per second for photochemical film (so shooting at, say, forty-eight frames per second) and projecting back at the standard twenty-four results in **slow motion.** (In this case the speed is reduced by half.) Slow motion is familiar from action films in which the technique draws out a car explosion or other dramatic action. Filming at a rate lower than the standard twenty-four (so at, say, eighteen frames per second) and projecting back at twenty-four results in **fast motion,** which has sometimes been put to comedic effect (although not so often anymore). Filming at one rate and projecting back at another is only one way to alter the speed of motion. It can also be done during post-production (after filming is completed) through analog as well as digital means.

Digital cinema technology facilitates a technique known as **ramping,** whereby the speed of motion changes over the course of a shot—from, say, normal to slow motion and back again. Or the film image might stop altogether through a technique known as a **freeze-frame.** In *Goodfellas* (Martin Scorsese, 1990), as we're being introduced to gangster Jimmy Conway, a shot of his face freezes while the film's narrator tells us that "Jimmy was one of the most feared guys in the city."

The Appearance of Depth

Because a film is moving photography, the lens attached to the camera has a bearing on the resulting image captured. One way this is true is through the sense of perspective and depth the image conveys. Depending on the lens used, a space—a bedroom, say—can be made to look as cavernous as a warehouse or it can seem to have almost no depth at all. Lenses have different focal lengths. The technical definition of this term doesn't concern us, as we're interested only in the results these lenses produce. (Again, we're concentrating on functions and effects, what's on the screen.) A **middle focal-length lens** (or normal lens) approximates what the human eye sees. So, if you were standing on a film set looking at two actors and then you looked through the lens, you wouldn't see much difference. But a lens can make the profilmic space (see chapter 3 on this term) look very different from what your eye would see.

Space captured with a **wide-angle lens** looks deeper than it really is, so this lens makes movement through depth appear faster, since a lunge through five feet that looks like ten will seem accelerated. The wider (aka the shorter) the lens, the greater the exaggeration of depth. If the lens is wide enough, the image can become visibly distorted, with straight lines in the setting curving around the center (**4.5–4.6**). This isn't generally a flattering lens to use on the human face, since it can make noses and other features look elongated and pronounced, even grotesque (**4.7**).

Conversely, a **telephoto lens** (or long lens) compresses the space. A long enough lens can make the space seem to telescope down to one

4.5 *2001: A Space Odyssey* (Stanley Kubrick, US/UK, 1968). A shot showing the space seen through a lens closer to a middle focal length . . .

4.6   . . . transitions to one filmed with an extreme-wide-angle lens.

depth (**4.8**). A football player on a field and the fans in the stands behind him can be made to appear the same size, even though they would look nothing like this if you were standing on the sidelines. Objects and persons at different depths can appear to be squashed onto the same plane.

There are fixed focal-length lenses, and there are ones that allow the focal length to be adjusted while filming. Changing the focal length over the course of a shot results in a **zoom,** in which the amount of space visible in the frame either increases or decreases. If the frame lets in

4.7 *Seconds* (John Frankenheimer, 1966). The distortion caused by an extreme-wide-angle lens conveys this drugged character's mental state.

4.8 *The Filth and the Fury* (Julien Temple, UK/US, 2000). A telephoto lens makes the horses seem closer to the standing man than they really are.

more space, this is a **zoom-out** (**4.9–4.10**). If the space decreases, this is a **zoom-in.** A zoom-in would change the view from a wide-angle image of, say, a crowded cafeteria to a telephoto image of just one person at a table.

Zooms can be easy to confuse with shots in which the framing changes by means of the camera physically moving forward or backward through space (discussed later in this chapter), but there are differences. You can usually tell by looking at elements in the frame. With zooming there

4.9 *Touching the Void* (Kevin Macdonald, UK/US, 2003). In this documentary, as we hear a man recall how isolated he and his climbing partner were on the mountain, . . .

4.10 . . . the camera zooms out until they all but disappear within the enormous landscape.

is no sense of moving through space, and the shots can have a static feel as they convey an impression of the camera merely photographically shrinking down (zooming out) or blowing up (zooming in) the image. With a zoom you can pick elements on different planes and notice that, no matter how much the framing changes, they never move in relation to each other. When the camera is moving through space, elements on different planes will separate as the camera pushes in and move closer together as it backs up.

Whether the camera is zooming or physically moving affects a viewer differently. Whereas a zoom conveys a sense only of seeing more or less space, a moving camera gives an impression of penetrating into or backing up *through space.* This can produce a more visceral sensation than a zoom. Sometimes a filmmaker will choose a zoom over a moving-camera shot simply because of budgetary or scheduling constraints, but this shouldn't stop us from asking how the technique is interacting with other elements in the shot, scene, and film.

If zooming produced identical results to moving the camera through space, then a forward moving camera and a zoom-out (or vice versa) should technically cancel each other out. But they do so only partially, and the result of combining these techniques, known as a **vertigo shot** (and sometimes a dolly zoom), can be strange and even hallucinatory. Alfred Hitchcock popularized this technique in *Vertigo* (1958), in which a character who is afraid of heights looks down a staircase, and the staircase seems physically to expand as it plunges into the depths. This shot combines a backward moving camera with a zoom-in. The resulting accordion-like warping of the space suggests this character's extreme anxiety.

Focus and Depth of Field

Filmmakers, like still photographers, manipulate *focus.* Elements in a shot that are in **focus** are crisply visible, while ones that are out of focus are blurry. In chapter 1, in the German TV commercial, the ghoulish figure is out of focus (**1.5**); and in the first *Down with Love* image the telephone is out of focus, and the woman is in focus (**1.24**). Everything in the *Touching the Void* images is in focus (**4.9–4.10**).

Filmmakers also control *depth of field,* which is something else that, along with the apparent depth, is affected by the type of lens selected. **Depth of field** refers to the thickness of the slab of space, parallel with the surface of the lens, wherein all elements will be in focus. Depth of field can run from very shallow (**4.11**) to very deep and even to infinity (**4.12**). One way filmmakers can direct viewer attention over the course

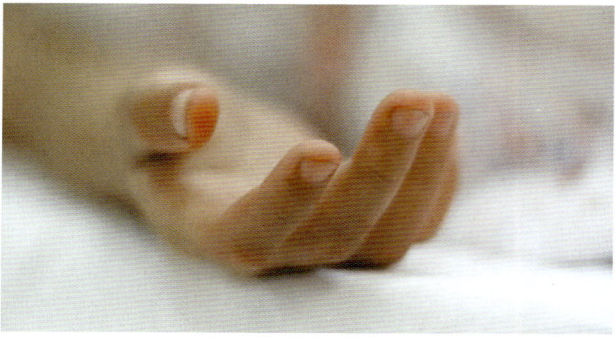

4.11 *The Killer* (John Woo, HK, 1989). An extremely shallow depth of field renders only the fingertips closest to the camera in focus.

4.12 *My Darling Clementine* (John Ford, 1946). Depth of field stretches to the horizon: everything, from the post nearest to the camera to the mountains in the far distance, is in focus.

of a shot is to limit the elements that are in focus, since we tend to look at what's in focus (although that's not the case with the German TV ad). Images captured with a wide-angle lens tend to have a greater depth of field, while ones captured with a telephoto lens tend to have a shallower one. Shots with a very extensive depth of field are called **deep-focus** shots. Chapter 3 refers to a technique called *deep-space staging*. You

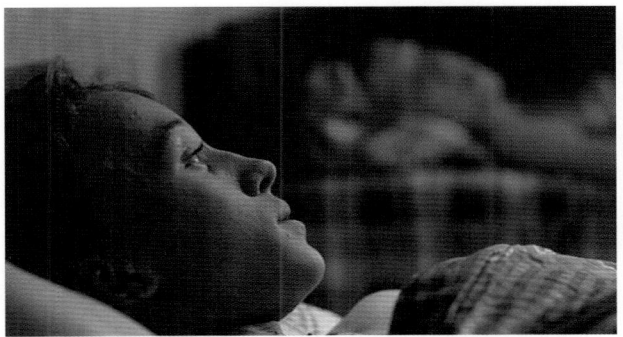

4.13 *The Return* (Andrey Zvyagintsev, Russia, 2003). Over the course of this shot, focus racks from the foreground figure . . .

4.14 . . . to the rear-ground figure.

may not be surprised to learn that deep-space staging and deep-focus cinematography frequently go hand in hand, although you can find instances of deep-space staging in which the figures move into and out of zones of fuzzy focus.

Filmmakers can use focus to cue viewers to change where they're looking over the course of a shot through a technique called **racking focus,** whereby the focus shifts from one plane to another (**4.13–4.14**). Racking focus can be viewed as an alternative to *cutting* from one element in a scene to another. (Editing is discussed in the next chapter.)

4.15 *Casablanca* (Michael Curtiz, 1942). Rear projection supplies the background.

4.16 *Star Wars: Episode IV–A New Hope.* Only the human figure and a small portion of the setting are physically real; the rest is a matte painting on glass.

Special Effects

The photographic nature of the shot allows for a range of **special effects** that further makes the film image unlike merely an arrangement of items in a box. The field of special effects has exploded in recent years, as digital technology has come to penetrate every part of the filmmaking process. What follows is the briefest overview of a few techniques.

An older technique is **superimposition,** in which elements filmed separately occupy the frame at the same time (**2.11** and **4.4**). Another is

4.17 In *John Adams* (Tom Hooper, 2008), computer effects multiply a handful of extras . . .

4.18 . . . into a crowd of ten thousand. Note also the digitally added background buildings.

rear projection (or rear-screen projection), a technique involving live elements such as actors in a car, a film screen, and a projector (**4.15**). The actors pretend to drive in front of the screen, on which is displayed a moving background image thrown onto it by a film projector behind. The meshing of foreground and rear ground is rarely convincing, but viewers accept it because it's a convention.

Another traditional way elements that have been filmed separately can be combined in a single shot is through **matte work,** in which live elements, typically actors and a small portion of a built set, are integrated with a background consisting of a matte painting (**4.16**). In the past, moving both live elements and mattes in an illusion of a single unified space could yield less than convincing results, when visible matte lines called attention to the artificial, collage-like nature of the image. In more recent films, **digital compositing** processes merge physical and computer-generated elements—including major characters such as Gollum in the *Lord of the Rings* and *Hobbit* movies—into seamless new realities undreamed of in decades past (**4.17–4.18**).

FRAMING THE IMAGE

Framing is hugely important for understanding the art of film, yet it's an elusive topic. It might not seem that important. It's just the *edges* of the image, right? No one talks about the edges of the *Mona Lisa.* But the ability to include elements in the frame, and, just as important, to exclude them—to *limit* what we see—constitutes one of the great powers available to filmmakers. The discussion of framing breaks into four parts: (1) *the frame's size and shape;* (2) *how framing determines whether objects exist in onscreen or offscreen space;* (3) *how framing can be described in terms of the camera's angle, level, height, and distance;* and (4) *how the frame can move relative to its contents.*

The Frame's Size and Shape

The frame's dimensions are in part determined by a film's **aspect ratio,** which is the ratio of the width of the image to its height. For decades the standard ratio for Hollywood films was 1.37:1. Called the **Academy ratio,** this frame is about a third (or 1.37 times) wider than it is tall, or roughly square. Over the years different **widescreen** technologies and formats have been introduced. A common ratio today is 1.85:1, a frame nearly twice as wide as it is tall. See the frame enlargement from *Casablanca* (**4.15**) for an example of the Academy ratio and the one from *Star Wars* (**4.16**) for an example of a widescreen image.

4.19 *Daughters of the Dust* (Julie Dash, US/UK, 1991). A masked frame shows us a point-of-view shot through a camera viewfinder—and shows the photographer something no one else in the scene can see, a mystical vision of an unborn child.

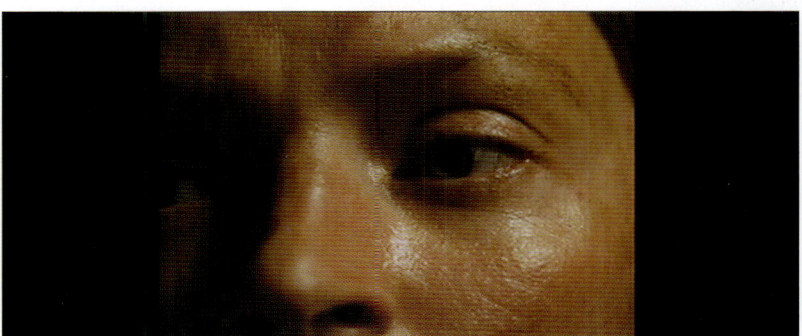

4.20 *Kill Bill: Vol. 2* (Quentin Tarantino, 2004). The widescreen image temporarily snaps down to a squarer shape to suggest the claustrophobic confinement of this captured character, who is about to be buried alive. (She escapes.)

A wide frame can pose challenges to a filmmaker who wants viewers to look where they need to in order to pick up salient information and keep pace with the story. Ways to address this challenge include shallow- and rack-focus techniques discussed above, lighting and staging (see chapter 3), moving the camera (discussed below), and using sound to direct the viewer's attention (see chapter 6).

4.21 *Phantom of the Paradise* (Brian De Palma, 1974). On the left side of the split screen a car explodes during the rehearsal of a musical number, while, on the right, the show's producer looks on.

A frame's size and shape may change over the course of a film. Segments of *The Dark Knight* (Christopher Nolan, 2008) were presented in some theaters on the huge IMAX screen. At certain moments the film transitioned from a widescreen format to a bigger size and the squarer ratio of 1.33:1. The frame's size and shape also can change temporarily when it's masked to simulate the view through a telescope or camera, or for other reasons (**4.19–4.20** and **2.7**).

A film also might show more than one discrete image simultaneously. A **split screen** divides the frame and presents two or more views, possibly of actions happening at the same time (**4.21**).

Another technique, an **iris-in,** begins a shot or scene with a small circle (or other shape) of visible image surrounded by black (or another color) that widens until it reveals the whole frame. The reverse, which might end a scene, is called an **iris-out.** Common in the silent era, irises are occasionally used today to evoke an older style of filmmaking or to add a self-consciously "artsy" touch.

Onscreen versus Offscreen Space

Chapter 2 noted that an element or action in a film can exist in onscreen or offscreen space. **Onscreen space** is space you can see on the screen.

4.22 *The Seventh Victim*
(Mark Robson, 1943).
A character, afraid she's
being stalked, pauses. Her
figure fills the lower-right
portion of the frame.

4.23 The face of a man emer-
ges from the shadows of
a doorway in the frame's
top-left quadrant, confirming her fears and balanc-
ing the composition.

Offscreen space is diegetic space outside the frame. An object or
person in offscreen space will be located beyond one of the four frame
lines (top, bottom, left, right), behind the camera, or behind the setting
(behind, say, a wall or tree). In the image from *Kill Bill: Vol. 2* (**4.20**), the
woman's feet are in offscreen space. Ways viewers can be alerted to
the presence of something in offscreen space include an onscreen character looking there, a sound coming from there (discussed in chapter 6),
and someone or something entering the frame.

A host of common strategies and practices for constructing on- and
offscreen space underpins the whole of narrative cinema, but different
sorts of films deploy these two kinds of space in distinctive ways. For
example, because what we can't see can be frightening, horror films
often load offscreen space with real and implied threats to the charac-

ters. A conventional strategy is to unbalance the frame. This is something even viewers who pay no attention to such things as composition will register as, on some level, they expect (or dread) that something will imminently enter the frame—a hand, an ax, a monster—to balance it (**4.22–4.23**).

Camera Angle, Level, Height, and Distance

The camera orients us to the contents of the frame through its *angle, level, height,* and *distance.* When a **camera angle** is **straight-on,** the camera points straight at a subject (**4.15**). A **low-angle** shot points up at a subject (**4.24**). A **high-angle** shot points down (**4.25**). A low-angle shot of a figure that towers over us can make the figure look powerful, and a high-angle shot can make a figure look diminutive and vulnerable, but whether this is the case will depend on the shot's context and on your own sense of what is going on in the shot, sequence, and film.

Camera level refers to whether the frame lines up with vertical and perpendicular lines in the setting. Most of the time the framing is **level,** but it can be skewed (**4.26**). This is called a **canted framing** (or Dutch angle). A canted framing can indicate that something going on in a shot is "off" in some way (supervillains are planning to take over the world, a character has just learned some terrible news, a city hall is mired in corruption). Or such a framing might mainly be used to load a composition with diagonals and render a shot more visually dynamic.

Camera height refers to the relative elevation of the camera. It runs from **high height** (**4.27**) to **medium height** (**4.28**) to **low height** (**4.29**).

It's worth pausing to stress that camera angle, level, and height can be easily confused. One term might seem to mean another. But while, for example, a shot filmed from a high height might also be a high angle (as in **4.27**), a shot filmed from low height can be a straight-on angle (as in **4.29**). Also, although in common usage, *level* might make us think of "height," in the language of formal analysis camera *level* and camera *height* are two different things. Make an effort to keep these terms straight, and this will help you sharpen your analysis as you look for ways

4.24 *Eternal Sunshine of the Spotless Mind* (Michel Gondry, 2004). A scene alternates low-angle shots . . .

4.25 . . . with high-angle shots.

4.26 *Batman* (Leslie H. Martinson, 1966). Canted framing in the supervillains' hideout.

4.27 *Ma vie en rose* (aka *My Life in Pink,* Alain Berliner, Belgium/FR/UK, 1997). High camera height (and also a high angle).

4.28 *Star Trek* (J. J. Abrams, 2009). Medium camera height. Also, note how this film, in which Kirk (center) is cast into a parallel universe in which he must fight to gain his rightful place in the captain's chair, signals, in its closing moments, the achievement of this hard-won equilibrium with this emphatically balanced composition.

4.29 *Seven Samurai* (Akira Kurosawa, JP, 1954). Low camera height (and also a straight-on angle).

4.30 *Tristana* (Luis Buñuel, SP/IT/FR, 1970). Extreme long shot.

4.31 *La strada* (Federico Fellini, IT, 1954). Long shot.

4.32 *The Immigrant* (Charles Chaplin, 1917). Medium long shot.

4.33 *Night and the City* (Jules Dassin, UK, 1950). Medium shot.

4.34 *The Help* (Tate Taylor, 2011). Medium close-up.

4.35 *Weekend* (Andrew Haigh, UK, 2011). Close-up.

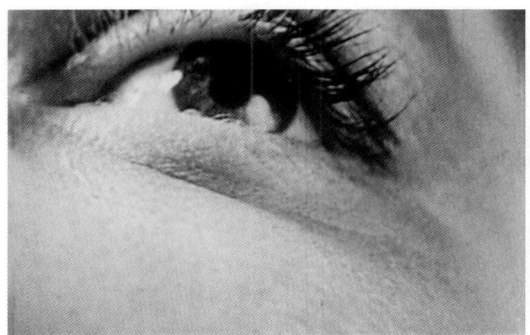

4.36 *Meshes of the Afternoon* (Maya Deren and Alexander Hammid, 1943). Extreme close-up.

these camera positions can combine in a single shot and how they can figure in patterns that stretch across sequences and whole films.

Finally, **camera distance** refers to how far away the camera is from its subject. While a shot can be of anything, the following terms are keyed to the human body. I will assign cutoffs more rigidly than filmmakers tend to, because in analysis it's important to be as accurate as possible. Some cutoffs you observe won't conform exactly to the ones given here. The important thing when applying these terms is to be as consistent as you can.

We run from *extreme long shot* to *extreme close-up.* In an **extreme long shot** the subject is far enough away to appear small in the frame (**4.30**) and can even be nearly swallowed up by the setting (as in **4.10**). In a **long shot** the whole figure fills the frame (**4.31**). A **medium long shot** cuts the figure off at the shins or knees (**4.32**); a **medium shot** at the waist (**4.33**); and a **medium close-up** at the chest (**4.34**). A **close-up** shows just the face, or a small object such as a pen or gun (**4.35** and **4.11**). An **extreme close-up** shows only a part of the face or small object (**4.36** and **4.20**).

Moving the Frame

Just as figures and objects can move within the frame (see chapter 3), the frame itself can move as well. Some aspect of the shot just discussed

4.37 *Tom Jones* (Tony Richardson, UK, 1963). The camera pans . . .

4.38 . . . left.

4.41 *Last Year at Marienbad* (Alain Resnais, FR/IT, 1961). As the woman walks forward, the camera tracks . . .

4.39 *Europa Europa* (Agnieszka Holland, GER/FR/
Poland, 1990). The camera tilts . . .

4.40 . . . down.

4.42 . . . backward.

4.43 *Marnie* (Alfred Hitchcock, 1964). The camera cranes
down, circling to the left . . .

4.44 . . . until it brings Marnie's face into view in a medium
close-up.

—camera angle, level, height, distance, or a combination—can change
over the course of a shot. Here we're talking mostly about camera movement, although zooming mobilizes the frame as well.

There are four types of camera movement. First is a **pan,** in which the
camera, without changing its physical location, swivels left or right
(**4.37–4.38**). With a **tilt** the camera, also from a fixed location, swivels
up or down (**4.39–4.40**). With a **tracking shot** (or dolly shot) the
camera moves over the ground forward, backward, to the left or right, in
a circle, or tracing some other pattern (**4.41–4.42**). A tracking camera

might be mounted on wheels or carried by hand. Last, with a **crane shot** the camera travels above the ground. It might be attached to a crane, handheld, or, less often, pointed out of an aircraft. In the shot in *Marnie* (**4.43–4.44**), for example, the camera drifts down and circles left until we see Marnie's face in a three-quarter frontal view. With a crane shot, camera *height* frequently changes. A crane may incorporate one or more of the other three movements. Also, as discussed in relation to vertigo shots earlier in the chapter, all four movements can combine with a zoom.

THE LONG TAKE

The next chapter will describe how editing can guide viewers in minute and effective ways. But a sequence or even a whole film can contain little or no editing. A shot of long duration is known as a **long take.** (Avoid confusing this term with a *long shot,* a designation of camera distance.) When a long take constitutes a whole scene, this is a **sequence shot.** Some admirers of the long take find built into the technique its own kind of suspense: viewers watch, and the shot doesn't end, and, on a level that might not be conscious, they begin to wonder what will have to happen before it does. A film can exploit this potential to increase the tension in a scene, turning the long take into a kind of pressure cooker that keeps building up steam until the chosen moment and manner of release—the bomb goes off, the couple kisses, or, as in the famous opening shot of *Touch of Evil* (Orson Welles, 1958), both of these things happen at the same time. A long take can make viewers feel trapped as they wait for the relief of a cut that will bring them to a different angle or new scene.

Like widescreen, a long take can make demands on filmmakers who want to keep viewers involved in the story and following along. Again, selective focus, lighting, staging, camera movement, and sound can assist not only in accomplishing these tasks but in creating virtuoso shots of extended duration.

A long take can compensate for a lack of cutting, and it can achieve aesthetic ends not possible through conventional editing techniques. For some—most notably French film critic André Bazin, who wrote in the 1940s and 1950s—one potential of the long take is a uniquely "cinematic" form of realism. In life there is no director slicing up reality into bite-size pieces and spoon-feeding them to us at precisely the moment when we're supposed to be paying attention to this or that detail. With a long take—especially one that refuses to come to our aid through staging, camera movements, and so on—we might miss the telling glance or tiny gesture that is the single most important thing going on in the whole, potentially busy, mise-en-scène. Without editing to spell out the connections and guide our attention, we might, if we're not paying attention—or don't know what to pay attention to—miss out, just like in real life.

The long take holds potentials impossible or difficult to realize through other means. Let's close by looking at an example of one of these extended duration shots.

A LONG TAKE IN *LETTER FROM AN UNKNOWN WOMAN*

Letter from an Unknown Woman (Max Ophüls, 1948) tells the story of a young woman, Lisa Berndle, who develops a crush on self-centered pianist Stefan Brand, who romances her as one of his many conquests and then promptly forgets her. She raises his son, harboring an unrequited love that makes her happiness impossible, and dies before Stefan can learn of her lifetime of waiting and devotion and of his own nearly total blindness to the same. He learns about both when, as the film begins, he receives a letter Lisa composed before dying. He starts reading, and a flashback begins that fills him (and us) in on Lisa's life in the shadows of his own. We learn of her encounters with Stefan over the years, one of which is at the opera, when Lisa, who has married to provide her son with a father, sees Stefan for the first time in ten years. The encounter is depicted through a long take.

The shot begins on a poster for the opera. Motivated by the movement of a couple standing next to the poster, the camera begins tracking right (**4.45**). We hear Lisa's voice as she reads from her letter: "The course of our lives can be changed by such little things. So many passing by, each intent on his own problems. So many faces that one might easily have been lost. I know now nothing happens by chance. Every moment is measured; every step is counted."

The couple exits the frame as the camera gracefully reverses direction to pick up the leftward movement of a threesome (**4.46**), then tracks right to follow a pair of military officers (**4.47**), then left to follow two women (**4.48**). This last movement brings the grand staircase into view. As we hear Lisa say, "every step is counted," she and her husband walk into the shot (**4.49**). They ascend the staircase, and the camera cranes up and to the right, following them to the top, where Lisa overhears a patron asking, "Isn't that Stefan Brand?" She comes to the balustrade and looks back down into the foyer (**4.50**). The long take ends with a cut to a point-of-view shot of Stefan below (**4.51**).

This long take dramatizes Lisa's perception of life both as it appears and as it really is. *So many passing by, so many faces.* This shot conveys a vibrant sense of contingency. One carefully framed shot after another, joined by editing, might seem to leave nothing to chance; but this crowded frame bustles with life as the sequence unfolds in a continuous stream of motion and activity. Visual details enter and exit the shot at every moment. Yet the sequence feels far from arbitrary or chaotic. The sinuously floating camera coordinates closely with the choreographed movements of the figures, gliding right, left, right, and left again. This is Vienna, and this gently swaying motion might call to mind the rhythm of a waltz. Without breaking the rhythm, the camera sweeps us and Lisa to the top of the stairs.

Nothing happens by chance. Every moment is measured; every step is counted. This complex shot seems to capture contingency when in fact everything was orchestrated before it began, like the machine that has caught Lisa up and will never let go. At the top of the stairs the answer to the question of what it will take to end this shot is answered

4.45 *Letter from an Unknown Woman.* The camera tracks right, . . .

4.46 . . . left, . . .

4.47 . . . right, . . .

4.48 . . . then left again, . . .

4.49 . . . picking up Lisa and
her husband.

4.50 The camera cranes up
and right as it follows
them to the top of the
stairs, where Lisa looks
down into the foyer.

4.51 Cut to a point-of-view shot of Stefan greeting two women on the steps below.

with a cut to Lisa's point of view of Stefan. If we wished, too, for her to see him again, we are satisfied—but in this film about endless longing and inevitable loss, our delayed satisfaction comes only in the form of more desire: from behind a column we look, and he remains at a distance. What seemed a chance encounter was in fact cruelly calculated, in this film by the long take and in Lisa's world by fate. The two meld together in the film's expressive style and careful use of a cinematic technique.

Editing

We've so far examined two of the four major components of film style and two ways of looking at the shot: mise-en-scène and cinematography. If all films consisted of a single shot and were silent, we'd be finished with our tour of film form now. But most films combine shots into patterns. They juxtapose images, and many films construct out of these combinations spatial and temporal wholes. And most films have sound. This chapter looks at how shots are combined, that is, at editing. The last chapter will consider film sound.

We have the shot, and as we've seen, there's a great deal going on within it. Yet much of what films *do,* what excites many people about them, is what happens when shots are combined. Below we look at some *editing basics* that can help you think about the editing in most any film. Then we consider two approaches to editing that we'll call *editing for continuity* and *editing for discontinuity.* We will keep historical considerations of these two styles to a minimum as we concentrate on how techniques associated with each one produce effects.

EDITING BASICS

We define **editing** as joining one shot with another. This is sometimes referred to as "cutting," but we'll prefer *editing* because editing doesn't necessarily involve physically cutting any film. **Editing in the camera,** for example, is accomplished by stopping the camera, changing whatever is in front of it, and starting it again. Digital editing systems also can render cutting unnecessary. Moreover, we'll define a *cut* not as two pieces of film that have been cut and spliced together but as one of four ways to join two shots.

Editing might seem a little like framing. Again, we're not talking about anything *in* the shots but rather the edges of the visible. Yet, also like framing, it would be hard to overstate the importance of editing for understanding and appreciating the art of cinema. In this section we consider two sets of four things. The first set is mechanical and concrete, the second more abstract. First, what are the *four types of edit* by which two shots can be joined? Second, what are *four ways editors can think about the relationship between two shots—that is, what qualities in them can they emphasize when joining the shots together?*

Four Kinds of Edit

We begin with the four kinds of join. The most common kind is a **cut,** by which Shot A instantly transitions to Shot B (**5.1–5.2**). Cuts are everywhere in films, and it might seem that nothing should be easier than seeing when one image changes into another in the blink of an eye. Yet cuts can be hard to spot. They can slip past unnoticed, even when one is consciously trying to count them. We consider why under "Editing for Continuity" below.

A second edit is a **fade-out/fade-in,** in which the image darkens until it becomes completely black (the fade-out), then lightens until the next shot is revealed (the fade-in). These transitions typically come between scenes and rarely happen within them. Often a fade-out/fade-in signals that some time has passed or that a major part of the film has ended and a new one is beginning. In *I Married a Monster from Outer Space* (Gene Fowler Jr., 1958), a bride kisses her husband on their wedding night. The scene ends with a fade-out. Then, following a fade-in, we see a close-up of a letter she's writing: ". . . our anniversary—but it has been a horrible year. I'm frightened and bewildered. Maybe it's me, but, oh, Mama, Bill isn't the man I fell in love with—He's almost a stranger."

Third is a **dissolve,** in which a shot gradually disappears while, superimposed over it, the next one gradually appears (**5.3–5.5**). A dissolve, too,

5.1 *The Dark Knight.* A shot transitions to the next . . .

5.2 . . . by means of a cut.

can signal a passage of time, but it generally does so less emphatically than a fade-out/fade-in can.

Last, with a **wipe** one shot gradually replaces another, as with a dissolve, but here the sense of overlap is crisper. A line—or an enlarging circle or diamond, or a shrinking shape, or a diagonal zigzag, etc.—moves across the screen, "wiping away" the first shot and replacing it with the second (**5.6–5.8**).

5.3 *Persepolis* (Vincent Paronnaud and Marjane Satrapi, FR/
US, 2007). A shot . . .

5.4 . . . dissolves . . .

5.5 . . . to a closer view. Dissolves within scenes are rare in
sound films.

5.6 *It Happened One Night* (Frank Capra, 1934). A woman waits in line for her turn to shower.

5.7 A vertical line wipes across the screen, right to left, . . .

5.8 . . . and reveals a new shot, in which some time has passed and the woman is exiting the shower building.

Four Kinds of Emphasis

The second set of four is more conceptual. Bordwell and Thompson describe four ways filmmakers can think about two shots when joining them together. Shots can be linked so that one or more kinds of relationships between them will be more or less salient. What kinds of relationships? An edit might emphasize *graphic qualities of the shots.* This juxtaposition conveys a sense of what's in the frame less as a represented space (an office, a baseball stadium) than as shapes and movements on a flat screen—objects in three dimensions resolved to two. So, for example, a beach ball makes an impression less as an inflated plastic sphere bouncing on sand than as a brightly colored circle against a yellow background. In this type of juxtaposition, shapes, tones, colors, and/or movements in one shot somehow play off ones in the preceding shot. A way they can do this is through a **graphic match,** which emphasizes *similarities* in the shapes, tones, colors, and/or movements in the two shots (**5.9–5.12**). Or shots can be joined to bring out graphic *contrasts,* to indicate, for example, that two characters are in conflict (one moves right; cut; the other moves left), or to create a sense of turbulent and even chaotic action on the screen. As with all four of these emphases, graphic similarities and dissimilarities can extend across many more than two shots, forming elaborate and complex patterns of development.

Second, a join can highlight *rhythmic qualities of the shots.* Here the editor concentrates on the shots' physical lengths. The silent experimental film *Cat's Cradle* (Stan Brakhage, 1959) consists of a series of images that include a wallpaper pattern, a woman's face (**5.13**), a bare foot, a cat (**5.14**), and a man smoking a cigarette. Many images are of discernibly real objects and persons, yet the editing scheme downplays the images' representational status. The editing mostly avoids drawing connections between these objects and persons in space and time. Instead, the images pulse on the screen, sometimes coming in staccato bursts so brief that it's hard to tell what we're seeing. Elsewhere the rhythm slows, and even though the longer-duration shot might be of an out-of-focus cat, it takes on weight and importance, and we look closely while we have the chance. Recurring images, like the wallpaper and

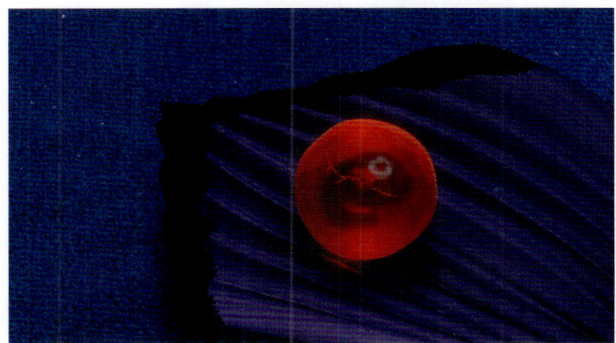

5.9 *Finding Nemo* (Andrew Stanton and Lee Unkrich, 2003). The prologue has presented the event that will launch and shape the arc of the film's narrative: a barracuda attack has left only one fish egg alive, damaged this egg, and killed the mother. Now the film has justified the situation we'll learn about after the opening credits: the clownfish father, who seemed a little neurotic before the disaster, is over-protective and has a horror of the dangers that could be-fall his slightly disabled son; and the son longs for inde-pendence and to be treated just the same as his friends. With the stage set for the adventure to come, a close shot of the lone egg dissolves . . .

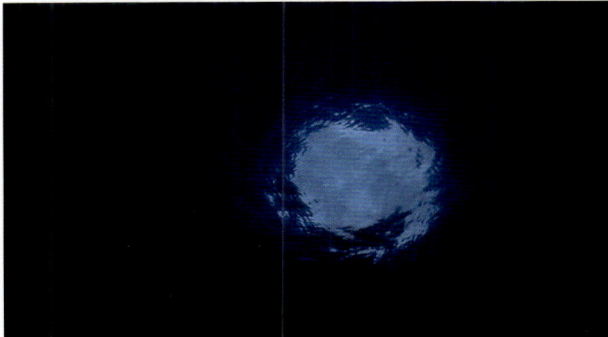

5.10 . . . to a graphic match of the moon shining through water, the background over which the title sequence begins.

5.11 In the Holocaust documentary *Night and Fog* (Alain Resnais, FR, 1955) the camera tracks rightward across a concentration camp's ruins, past fence posts that slide *right to left.*

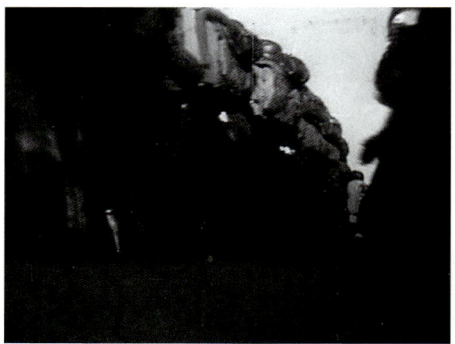

5.12 Cut to archival footage of a stationary camera shot of Nazis marching *right to left,* in columns that mesh with the movement and shapes of the posts slipping past in the preceding shot. The contrast from color to black and white is stark, but the graphic *continuities* that bridge the transition are one of the ways this film implicitly suggests that the Nazi threat will never be completely vanquished as long as we continue to think that it could never happen again.

5.13 *Cat's Cradle.* Two recurring images, in this rapidly and rhythmically edited six-minute film, are of a woman . . .

5.14 . . . and a cat.

bare foot, form motifs that unify the film, even while the film resists interpretations that would try to pin down its meaning. *Cat's Cradle* unfolds as a fantasia of pure rhythm and shape, a lyrical film poem.

Rhythmic qualities might be emphasized in a narrative film as well, in a scene of growing tension, for example. Imagine a western gunfight in which, as the scene progresses toward closer views—from extreme long shots of the two men to extreme close-ups of their eyes and hands —the shots grow shorter until, in an explosion of very brief shots, the men fire. The action proceeds in real time (a second of story time equals a second of screen time), but rhythmic cutting accelerates the pace as the scene nears its climax.

Third, editing can emphasize *spatial qualities of the shots.* A filmmaker can link shots with the aim of constructing a spatial whole, one that's entirely synthetic and manufactured yet that we perceive to be seamless—even though the seams are quite visible. How films accomplish this is described under "Editing for Continuity" below.

And finally, editing can emphasize *temporal qualities of the shots.* This is editing that conveys a sense of time as the characters experience it. In films, time usually progresses from one shot to the next in linear fashion. Chapter 2 noted two exceptions: flashbacks and flashforwards. A film might also omit some story time between shots through a device called an **ellipsis.** The images from *It Happened One Night* (**5.6–5.8**) show an example of an ellipsis, a technique that can be accomplished through a wipe, fade-out/fade-in, dissolve, or cut. An ellipsis might conceal crucial story information to be revealed later, although more commonly, it just skips over some unexciting material as it moves the film along at an agreeable pace. A woman sits on her bed tying her running shoes. Cut. She closes her front door and starts her run. Viewers know some diegetic time has been snipped out, and they barely register this as the story carries them along.

Some films use ellipses in more noticeable ways, ones that can disturb a viewer's sense of closely following a story, as the editing seems to be "sliding around" important events, omitting things that should not be omitted, leaving viewers to infer major plot points, and possibly never confirming or disconfirming their guesses. A film with this sort of highly **elliptical editing** style is *No Country for Old Men* (Joel and Ethan Coen, 2007). This film kills off a major character, when it had made no indication that this development was imminent, then shows us only the aftermath. Elsewhere, it cuts away from a tense scene before the scene has fully played out, and viewers can only wonder exactly how—and even whether—another major character dies. The choice to leave these gaps unfilled yields provocative results, for the film's refusal to answer questions it pointedly raises—and to indulge the thirst for righteous killing that Hollywood films (and especially westerns, which *No Country* evokes throughout) typically whip up and satisfy—encourages us to take a distanced and reflective stance on the material. *No Country* inclines us to ask how violence often works in mainstream movies and how viewers are routinely implicated in a production-and-consumption feedback cycle that counts on their dollars to keep turning.

Rarer than ellipses is **overlapping editing,** which extends screen duration by repeating the action seen at the end of a shot at the start of the next. Several shots might be stacked in this manner, creating a stuttering effect. Overlapping editing can be viewed as an alternative to slow motion (see chapter 4), because both techniques lengthen screen duration. A boldly experimental cinema movement of the 1920s, Soviet Montage (discussed later in this chapter), employed overlapping editing to punch up the energy of diegetic actions and for other purposes. A mainstream narrative film can do the same in, for example, a scene of spectacular action such as an explosion. The explosion might have been filmed with several cameras, allowing the editor to cut from one angle to another, overlapping the action to heighten and prolong the spectacle. We'll look at an example of overlapping editing later in this chapter.

Some final thoughts on these four emphases. First, these areas overlap all the time. The shots from *Night and Fog* (**5.11–5.12**) create a graphic match, and they also bridge two times. *Cat's Cradle* (**5.13–5.14**) streams a pulsating cascade of images past us, the graphic interplay of which cannot be separated from the film's rhythmic editing. Our hypothetical gunfight example emphasizes rhythmic qualities while also constructing a spatial and temporal whole. Which qualities you highlight in your analysis will depend on the sequence and on what you want to say.

Second, these four qualities might seem straightforward, but it's easy to confuse them, especially *graphic* with *spatial* and *rhythmic* with *temporal.* For both these pairs of emphases it might help to think of the difference between the first and second term as that between seeing the screen as a *surface on* which graphic and rhythmic relationships are playing out versus seeing it as a *window through* which we watch spatial and temporal relationships unfolding. Look for ways these four areas overlap and interact—in pairs of shots, in longer sequences, and across whole films.

Last, I risk oversimplification in saying this, but in commercial narrative cinemas such as Hollywood's, spatial and temporal qualities come to the fore, while avant-garde and experimental cinemas such as Soviet Montage give greater prominence to graphic and rhythmic qualities. We consider these two movements next.

TWO APPROACHES TO EDITING

Editing has built into it a potential to disrupt. The term *cut* implies this. What is being cut? The flow of action, the wholeness of the unbroken shot. A filmmaker can exploit this potential to achieve certain ends or downplay it to achieve others. We start with the second of these two possibilities.

Editing for Continuity: Classical Hollywood Cinema

A major style of filmmaking is **continuity editing.** Also known as "classical continuity," this is a style strongly associated with classical Hollywood cinema, which was developed and perfected during the studio era of Hollywood cinema history. Classical continuity outlived the studio era, is still much in use today, and has spread to cinemas around the world. So this is an enormously influential approach to editing. Continuity editing isn't just editing; it's a whole system with editing at its center.

Continuity editing is easy to understand but hard to analyze. Why? "Continuity editing" might seem like a contradiction in terms. Editing is fundamentally a *breaking* of continuity. We'll see later on in the chapter that for some filmmakers this capacity of the cut to disrupt is what gives editing its kick. Editing can be abrasive, but if the main goal is to tell a story, a filmmaker might not want this. If the aim is for the viewers' absorption into a world that seems complete and present and whole, one where events are linked by cause and effect and seem to unfold naturally in time and space, then something has to be done about the power of the cut to undermine this objective.

To this end, Hollywood filmmakers developed a system that is sometimes referred to as "invisible editing." With it they create films that, though held together by visible seams, somehow appear seamless. How do they do this? It has to do with the dominance of story. Continuity editing is founded on the idea that the main thing a film should do is tell a story—deliver the information, the emotions, a certain orientation to the material. And because this is the priority, an importance is placed on the smoothness of transitions. Because the goal is to channel the viewers' attention into the story, the discontinuity of a cut has to be tamed, covered over by a continuity, a consistency, one that bridges space and time. One must tap tendencies in viewers, both hardwired and conditioned into them (in large measure by watching movies), that will make them willing accomplices to the illusion.

The 180-degree system. The story flows over the cuts. We can think about how this happens in terms of space, and here we come to the core structuring principle of continuity editing, the **180-degree system,** which centers on what is known as the **180-degree line** (or the axis of action). This is a line that appears nowhere in the setting or onscreen, yet everything in the way the shots are assembled revolves around it. It's an imaginary line connecting the two most important elements in the scene at a given moment. The easiest way to picture this line is in a scene involving two people facing each other and having a conversation. The 180-degree line would connect these people.

Here's how it works. Picture a scene showing this conversation. Imagine you're viewing the space from above, straight down. Draw a line that runs through the heads of the two people. Pick one side of this line. On this side, draw a half-circle that begins at one end of the line and terminates at the other. Suppose you want to film Person A. Place the camera anywhere inside your half circle and film that person—long shot, close-up, low angle, whatever you decide. Now you want a shot of Person B. Place the camera anywhere you want—*as long as it's inside your half circle.* This is important, and here's the whole point of the 180-degree system, because staying inside this semicircle keeps

screen direction consistent. When screen direction stays consistent, people who are supposed to be looking at each other will appear to be looking at each other. One looks *right*. Cut. The other one is looking *left*.

Shooting Person A from inside the semicircle and then moving outside it to film Person B would break continuity and constitute, within this system, an error. It's called "crossing the line," and the resulting problem is that now the two people appear not to be looking at each other (one right and the other left) but at the same thing (both, say, to the right). And someone crossing a room will seem suddenly to have reversed directions. The result can be a blip of spatial disorientation for a viewer, something editors working on mainstream films typically try to avoid. I say "typically" because sometimes a filmmaker will cross the line deliberately to, for example, intensify the frenetic feel of a car chase or for other purposes.

Continuity devices. This is the 180-degree system broadly defined. Within it are a series of devices, special kinds of shots and shot combinations that are so useful and routine that they have names. These devices are better thought of as guidelines than as rules because, as supple and flexible as they are, filmmakers can violate and even abandon them when they have reason to. Still, most of the time, filmmakers follow this system. Let's look at the devices within it. The next several illustrations come from a scene in the western *Stagecoach* (John Ford, 1939), in which a band of travelers has stopped to have a meal and vote on whether to continue on with the journey, which would cross through dangerous Indian territory.

First is an **establishing shot,** which shows us more or less the whole space wherein a scene will unfold (**5.15**). This is the space that the ensuing shots will carve into closer views. An establishing shot might begin a scene, be delayed by a shot or more, or, especially in more recent films, be omitted altogether. When they appear, establishing shots provide a "map" of the space viewers can keep in mind as the scene plays out. A **reestablishing shot** might appear later in the scene (**5.16**). If an establishing shot provides a mental map, a reestablishing shot

5.15 *Stagecoach.* Characters take up positions in the space as the scene presents an establishing shot.

5.16 Later in the scene, as the travelers sit down to eat, we see a reestablishing shot.

refreshes the map and might show a smaller—or overlapping but slightly different—portion of the space, one that takes in just the area wherein the rest of the scene will unfold.

A useful device for representing a conversational exchange is **shot/ reverse shot,** in which, from the same side of the 180-degree line, the scene alternates views of the characters (**5.17–5.18** and **4.24–4.25**). Within the classical continuity system any such alternation, whether or not each shot is of a character, is called a **reverse angle** (or reverse shot; also see **4.5–4.6**). Staying on the same side of the line maintains screen direction. In a shot/reverse shot exchange, the shoulder of the rear-facing figure in the foreground might or might not be visible. The depicted interaction need not be a conversation. It could be a fight, or, as in the example from *Stagecoach,* an exchange of glances.

5.17 In this shot/reverse shot alternation the first character looks offscreen right . . .

5.18 . . . and the second looks offscreen left, making the women appear to be looking at each other.

Most often with shot/reverse shot editing, the characters are looking at each other. When they are, the exchange consists of a bundle of *eyeline matches,* which is another device in the continuity editor's tool kit. With an **eyeline match** Shot A shows a character looking offscreen, and then Shot B shows what the character is looking at. In *Stagecoach* the rear-facing figure in the center of the frame looks right (**5.19**). Cut to a shot that shows us where he's looking (**5.20**). In this pair of shots (as in **5.17–5.18**) the second one isn't a point-of-view shot—that is, a view from the spatial standpoint of the person looking in the first shot. Eyeline matches *can* be point-of-view shots, though, and so they can increase the subjectivity of the narration as discussed in chapter 2.

This scene also contains a **match on action,** in which an action begun in one shot is completed in the next (**5.21–5.22**). This is a contin-

5.19 The speaking character (center, back to us) looks offscreen right.

5.20 Cut to an eyeline match that joins the two spaces and establishes where the characters are in relation to each other. Note that this shot reveals a portion of the space not seen in the establishing shot (**5.15**).

uity device because it "tricks" viewers into watching the diegetic action rather than being distracted by the artificial, pasted-together quality of the scene. Our attention to the action carries us across the edit without our feeling the bump.

Let me stop to highlight an area of possible confusion. We have so far encountered the terms *graphic match, eyeline match,* and now *match on action.* Notice how similar these terms are. It's easy to mix them up. Taking a moment now to review what each one means will help you keep them straight later on.

A scene may include a **cheat cut,** in which a small degree of continuity is sacrificed to achieve some end. This might be to serve a requirement of the narrative. Say two people will kiss in a scene, but the heights of the actors differ considerably. With the cut to a medium close-up, the

5.21 The speaking figure (his coat draped over his arm) starts to raise his hand.

5.22 Cut to a match on action as he completes the gesture. We watch the gesture, not the cut.

shorter one (now standing on a box) will suddenly be tall enough for the two to kiss without the action looking awkward. Then, with the cut back to a more distant view, the actor will have just as instantly returned to his or her true height. Or the motivation might be aesthetic. Suppose a character sits at a desk in Shot A, and the gooseneck lamp next to his head looks fine. But with the cut to Shot B, a closer view, the top frame line cuts the lampshade in half in a way that makes the composition look ragged. The head of the lamp will be squashed down a couple of inches before the second shot is filmed. Attentive viewers might notice this minor change in the mise-en-scène but also might not care. Most viewers probably won't notice at all. If the story is sufficiently engaging, this sort of adjustment will be something else that, along with the cuts, recedes into the background of the viewing experience.

It's easiest to locate the 180-degree line in a two-person scene in which the line doesn't move. But a scene can have several characters in it, and the line can move at any time. In a scene with more than two people, the line typically connects the two most important characters at that moment, as the *Stagecoach* images suggest. Ways to change the line once it has been established include cutting away to something—a clock on the mantle, something happening across town—then returning to the action, giving the filmmaker a chance to draw the line between a different set of elements; putting the camera *on* the line; moving the characters around in the space; or, possibly in combination with moving the characters, moving the camera. Filmmakers have many options to choose from as long as they keep the space legible.

The *Stagecoach* scene is also a good one for demonstrating that these are guidelines and not rules. At one point in the scene, in Shot A (**5.23**) the man looks *left* at the woman. Cut to Shot B (**5.24**), where the woman looks *right* at the man. The camera has stayed within the semi-circle. But in Shot C (**5.25**) the man is looking *right*. Nothing has led us to suspect that he moved while she was speaking or that any time has elapsed between Shots B and C. Screen direction has not been kept consistent: the camera has crossed the line. If you watch for it, you'll notice that films will occasionally do this without very noticeable consequences.

These devices all preserve continuity within a circumscribed space such as a room or other localized setting. But sometimes a film will spread the viewers' attention over a wider area. A common practice is to interweave something happening at one location with something happening at another. A film might cut between two or more locations many times within even a short span of screen time. This practice is called **parallel editing** (and sometimes crosscutting), wherein shots are intercut so that viewers understand, or suspect, that two or more lines of action are related and, in most cases, happening at the same time (**5.26–5.27**). Earlier in the chapter, we considered how editing can emphasize temporal relations among shots. Parallel editing does this when it asserts the simultaneity of two or more lines of narrative development.

5.23 Shot A. The man in the foreground looks *left*. Also, note this instance of aperture framing (see chapter 3), which places emphasis on the background figure, a major character in the film.

5.24 Shot B. The woman looks *right*. The cut preserves screen direction.

5.25 Shot C. The man looks *right*. The camera has crossed the 180-degree line.

5.26 *Broken Blossoms* (D. W. Griffith, 1919). Parallel editing intercuts a scene of a man brutalizing his daughter . . .

5.27 . . . with shots of her protector searching for her. D. W. Griffith pioneered this technique in narrative cinema.

The prototypical application of parallel editing is a character racing on horseback to rescue another one who is tied up on train tracks. Such a sequence might intercut *three* lines of action: shots of the figure on the horse; shots of the figure on the tracks; and shots of the train bearing down on the spot at which the other two lines will converge, hopefully before the train gets there. This technique vividly communicates all the information viewers need, underscoring the relevant spatial, temporal, and causal connections (remember the definition of *narrative* from chapter 2) required for a viewer's swift, and even breathless, narrative uptake. As this illustration shows, parallel editing is a powerful tool for construct-ing suspenseful sequences (see chapter 1), as viewers have but one question *(Will the character be reached in time?)* and one expectation *(The character will, but we have to wait for it to happen)*. We can note, parenthetically, that a much less common alternative to parallel editing is a split screen, a device that also may show two or more concurrent actions (as in **4.21**).

One last continuity device, really a bundle of devices, is a **montage,** which is a sequence that represents a process (falling in love, training for the big fight, growing from a child to an adult) or, less often, a character's agitated mental state (madness, a drug-induced hallucination, an epiphany that triggers a flood of realizations). Montages that represent a process rely heavily on ellipses, as they can cover a significant amount of story time in just a couple of minutes of screen time. When a montage starts, a film's style typically becomes more overt and self-conscious. Diegetic sounds usually drop away and are replaced by nondiegetic music (maybe a pop song), and the sequence can feature a number of wipes, dissolves, graphic matches, slow motion, and other showy stylistic devices. When the montage ends, diegetic sound returns in full, and the flow of time slows to its former pace.

Editing for Discontinuity: Soviet Montage

Editing is a great storytelling tool, but along with editing comes a potential for disruption. Fundamentally, to cut is to break the visual flow. Hollywood developed strategies for coping with this, while other practices looked for ways to harness the cut's volatile power, including ones that would direct its energy back into the stories they were telling. The most important practitioner of this approach was Sergei Eisenstein, a film theorist and also the central filmmaker in the **Soviet Montage** school of the 1920s. *Montage* is this movement's word for *editing*. (We distinguish this Montage from the Hollywood kind by capitalizing Eisenstein's.) Through Montage these filmmakers aimed to achieve ends that differed from the ones sought after by most working within the Hollywood tradition.

The Montage of attractions. Eisenstein described what he called the "attraction," which he envisioned as a "molecular" entity that could be joined with other entities to form combinations that were greater than the sum of their parts. He developed this idea before he made his first film, when he was working in theater, but when he got to the cinema, he excitedly began to think about the shot—this basic building block of cinema—as a molecular entity that could be combined and recombined in new and powerful ways. He advocated editing shots to produce maximum conflict. Not just between shots but within them, he felt, one should seek to create clashes. Through Montage one should join shots of contrasting lengths, as well as ones bringing together jangling mixtures of movements, tones, and scales. These, recall from earlier in the chapter, are rhythmic and graphic qualities of the shots. So follow a shot of something small and white with one of something big and dark, and a shot of something moving to the right with one of something moving to the left. Maximum contrast, conflict, and collision—Eisenstein believed that stirring up viewers through such juxtapositions would lead them to revelatory insights about the true nature of such things as labor, capital, and society and inspire them to revolutionary action.

Discontinuity devices. Eisenstein's was a political cinema. Filmmakers can use editing to absorb viewers, drawing them into a story, or to bring audiences to their feet in outrage or some other state of wide-eyed awareness. And a single film can elicit both these sorts of responses, as Eisenstein's did, for he told rousing stories, too. At the climax of his first film, *Strike* (USSR, 1925), striking workers are put down by armed soldiers. In the midst of the bloody massacre, the film intercuts images of a bull being slaughtered (**5.28–5.29**). This bull is not part of the diegetic action. It seems to exist outside the space and time of the film. There's something abstract about its presence, and one can't help but wonder on what thematic (versus narrative) grounds this presence can be justified. One possibility is that the film is paralleling the heartlessly efficient slaughter of the strikers with that of this animal. This sort of interpolated image, called a **nondiegetic insert,** rather than producing continuity, comes across as a form of explicit commentary that has been wedged into the action to make a point.

A second device associated with this cinema is the **jump cut.** Pio-

5.28 *Strike.* The sequence intercuts the massacre of the strikers . . .

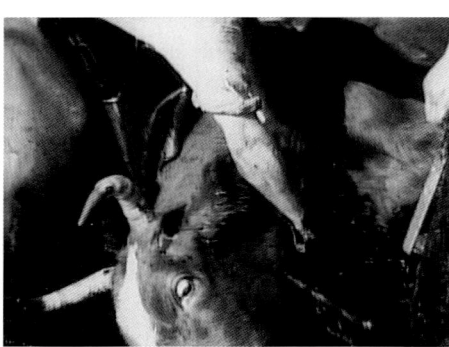

5.29 . . . with nondiegetic inserts of a bull being slaughtered.

neered by Eisenstein, and revived in later cinemas—notably the French New Wave in the late 1950s and 1960s—this technique involves changing the image from one shot to the next but not changing it enough for the second shot to register as simply a different view of the ongoing action. The shots are sufficiently alike to make the image appear to "jump" on the screen. In Eisenstein's most famous film, *Battleship Potemkin* (USSR, 1925), a sleeping sailor is struck by a callous officer (**5.30– 5.31**). Directly on the lashing action the film cuts to a closer view, instantly magnifying the onscreen expanse of the sailor's back. This edit works differently than does a match on action, in which the lash would carry across the cut and make the cut less noticeable. Instead, not only the sailor but the film itself seems to respond to the officer's strike. The cut temporarily "ruptures" the film's surface, encouraging viewers to

5.30 *Battleship Potemkin.* As an officer whips a sailor, . . .

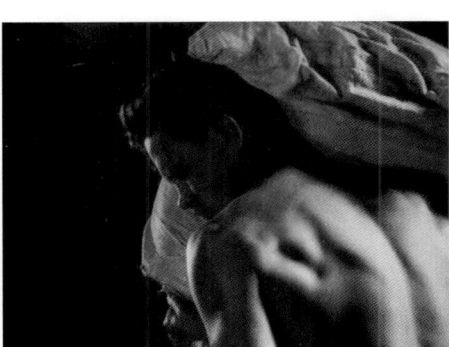

5.31 . . . the film jump-cuts to a closer view.

experience a sympathetic response to the persecution they are witnessing. The diegetic action is mirrored in the cut as the whole film seems momentarily to recoil with the pain and injustice of this violent outburst.

Then the sailor reacts. Diegetically, it's not much of an action: he turns and lifts himself up slightly (**5.32–5.33**). But, over two shots, this action is partially repeated. This is through a third discontinuity device, one we encountered earlier in the chapter, *overlapping editing.* Recall that overlapping editing stretches the duration of an action in a more abrupt fashion than slow motion does. It's hard to watch an instance of overlapping editing and not think about the editing. Yet this overlap in *Potemkin* doesn't take us out of the moment. It underlines it. Why do so? Possibly because this action—"rising up"—bears significance as,

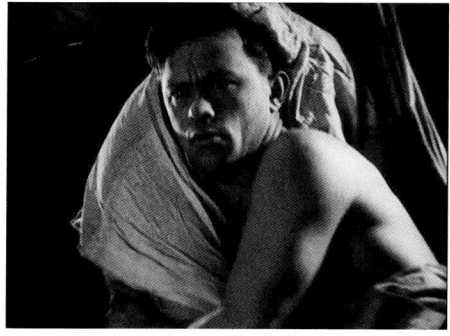

5.32 The sailor turns to face the officer.

5.33 Overlapping editing shows this action twice.

metaphorically, the very thing toward which all of the indignity and suffering shown in this film must, under a Marxist worldview, inevitably lead.

Potemkin seized the raw materials of both the profilmic world and the film medium itself and transformed them in ways that audiences around the world found electrifying. Here was a power that had no corollary in the theater or any other medium. Lovers of cinema, and filmmakers of political and other stripes, championed Eisenstein and Soviet Montage for the revolutionary potentials they discovered and unleashed in cinematic form. In contrast to André Bazin (see chapter 4), who felt that it was by *not* cutting that the cinema fulfilled its destiny, Eisenstein and his fellow filmmakers embraced editing as a means to stir viewers to new heights of consciousness and action.

Some Final Thoughts on These Two Approaches

We find striking contrasts between Hollywood and Soviet Montage films, but we also see similarities. For one thing, both focus intently on viewers. It is the anticipation of their responses that drives most every choice the Hollywood and Montage practitioner makes. For another, editing figures prominently at the center of both practices. And last, Eisenstein doesn't hesitate to appropriate Hollywood "tricks" to manipulate viewers' emotions. In *Potemkin*'s most famous sequence, one of the most famous in cinema history, the Odessa Steps sequence, Cossacks turn a sunny day in a port city into a bloody melee. After a mother is cut down, her baby rolls in its carriage down the long flight of stone steps and through the thick of the massacre. We fear for this child just as we would an imperiled child in a standard Hollywood melodrama.

Montage films can look like Hollywood films, and Hollywood films are just as free to borrow from Montage films. I close with an example of the latter.

EDITING IN A SEQUENCE FROM *PSYCHO*

Forty-six minutes into *Psycho* (Alfred Hitchcock, 1960), the character we've been following up to this point steps into the shower. Then, in one of the most famously shocking sequences in the history of the movies, she is murdered by a barely seen assailant (**5.34–5.39**). The sequence presents a dizzying display of concussive edits, a barrage of shots that, Hitchcock boasted, never show the knife actually making contact with the victim. (It does in one shot.) The gruesome violence depicted in the sequence is impossible to separate from the editing scheme. The onslaught of extremely brief shots, from a host of angles, and including many disjointedly close-up views, spans only a couple of minutes of screen time.

The first three images (**5.34–5.36**) show examples of **axial cutting,** which is cutting along a line to a more distant or closer view of a subject. This produces a jump cut, as we saw when the sailor is struck in *Potemkin*. Axial cutting violates a Hollywood rule of thumb known as

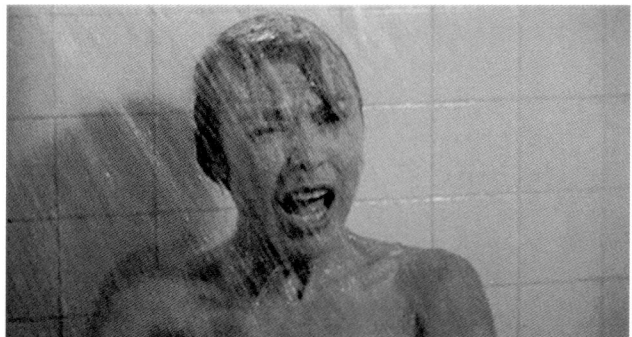

5.34 *Psycho.* On the character's scream the camera jump-cuts . . .

5.35 . . . to a closer view . . .

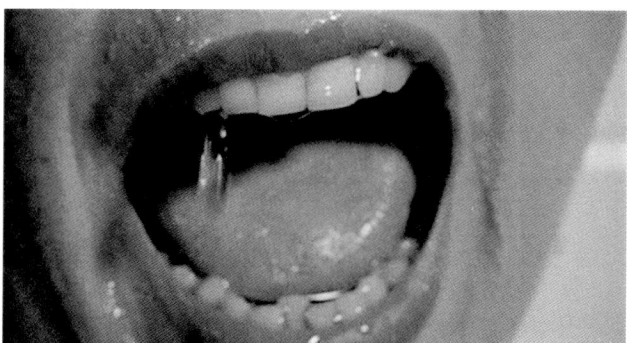

5.36 . . . twice.

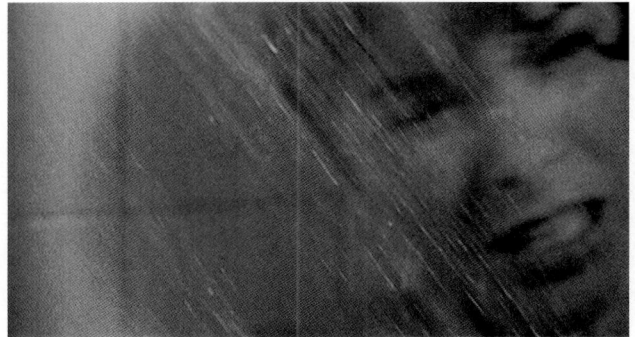

5.37 Three consecutive shots, in the flurry that follows, . . .

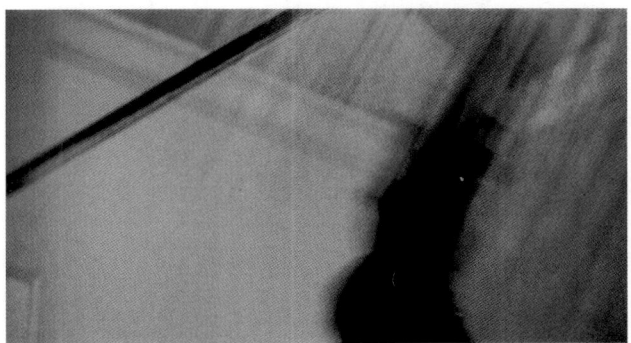

5.38 . . . show how this sequence splinters the space, . . .

5.39 . . . rendering it nearly abstract.

the thirty-degree rule, according to which, when cutting from a shot of something to a different shot of the same, one should vary the camera-to-subject axis by at least thirty degrees. Otherwise the second shot won't look sufficiently different from the first, and the image will appear to hiccup, or convulse, on the screen. These jump cuts combine with the character's scream to telegraph her terror as she watches her attacker draw back the knife for the first of many strikes.

Psycho sets out to agitate its viewers profoundly, and not just by turning the narrative in a shocking direction following almost none of the conventional warnings. Similar to *Potemkin*'s release of cinematic energy at the moment of the officer's lash, this sequence harnesses filmic cutting to intensify a killer's cutting. Hollywood films routinely blunt the abrasive power of the cut, but they don't have to.

Sound

6

Form in story films consists of narrative and style, with style consisting of four components, the last of which is sound. As I noted about framing and editing, there's something elusive about sound. Framing and editing exist at the margins of the visible. Sound is even harder to study. It's not even visible. And we are a visually oriented culture. When we mean "Do you understand?" we often ask, "Do you see?" And we have the expression "Seeing is believing." People bring to films a deeply ingrained focus on the visual. This has led to a tendency to neglect film sound, although this has begun to change in recent decades.

Much of what follows proceeds from a distinction we know, that between diegetic and nondiegetic elements. There is *diegetic sound* and *nondiegetic sound.* **Diegetic sound** is understood by viewers to originate in the story world. A film shows a bird alighting on a branch and starting to sing. We hear the warbling. This birdsong is a diegetic sound. Now imagine a scene in which two people sit at an outdoor café. Among the ambient sounds heard in the background is birdsong. We can't see the bird, but this sound, too, is diegetic because we understand its source to be within the diegesis. **Nondiegetic sound** comes from outside the story world. The most common kind is **nondiegetic music.** In the shower scene in *Psycho* (see chapter 5) an orchestral score consisting solely of stringed instruments piercingly accompanies the action. No one in the scene can hear this music because it is nondiegetic. Nondiegetic music is one way films can bypass our intellects and speak directly to our emotional selves. Stabs of violins will make us tense up during a scary scene whether or not we think the movie is any good. Music works with narrational and other techniques we have discussed to make film viewing a more deeply felt experience.

A sound film also might incorporate *silence* for dramatic or other purposes. A scene rife with visual activity and sound that grows suddenly quiet and still can make us feel a surge of expectation as we wait for something to occur that will break the uneasy calm. This is what happens in *The Matrix,* in the moments before Neo and Smith draw their guns (**1.1**). Asking questions about how sound and silence interact with the image will bring you to richer understandings of how films tell stories and work their effects.

DIEGETIC SOUND AND SPACE

Sticking with diegetic sound, let's revisit our distinction between onscreen and offscreen space (see chapters 2 and 4). Diegetic sound can relate in different ways to what we see in the frame. It can be **onscreen sound.** This means viewers understand a sound to be emanating from a source visible on the screen, like the bird on the branch in my first example above. If the sound's purported source is onscreen, then whether the bird, person, bus, or whatever made the sound and a microphone picked it up, or whether the sound was added during postproduction, it's an onscreen sound. Bugs Bunny chomps a carrot and says, "What's up, Doc?" The rabbit, we know, is not making the chomping noises or doing the talking, but because we understand Bugs to be making these sounds, they are onscreen sounds. It's how viewers construe a sound that matters for our definition and not any fact of a film's production. When viewers understand the source of a diegetic sound to be outside the screen space, like the background birdsong in my café example, this is an **offscreen sound.** Does it make sense to speak of onscreen or offscreen *non*diegetic sound? No, because nondiegetic sound exists in a different realm from the story world altogether. It is neither onscreen nor offscreen.

Offscreen sound is one way films can alert us to the presence of offscreen space and to things in it. Another, recall from chapter 4, is when a character looks offscreen. Here's an illustration of both of these

6.1 *The Devil Rides Out.* The character hears noises, . . .

6.2 . . . rushes to a closet, flings open the doors, looks down . . .

6.3 . . . and sees a basket of chickens.

possibilities. In *The Devil Rides Out* (Terence Fisher, UK, 1968) a character suspects that he is in a house where devil worship is being practiced. He hears clucking sounds (**6.1**). These are offscreen sounds. He rushes to a closet, throws open the doors, and looks down into offscreen space (**6.2**). What he sees, chickens to be used for a Black Mass ceremony (**6.3**), confirms his suspicions.

We've so far built on our distinctions between nondiegetic and diegetic elements and between onscreen and offscreen space. Here now is a technique associated with diegetic sound, a **dialogue overlap,** which is a line of dialogue that continues across a cut that falls within a scene. This device is part of the continuity editor's tool kit (see chapter 5), because viewers listening to a character talking will be less inclined to notice a cut. Editors exercise enormous flexibility when constructing a dialogue scene, for at any moment they may show the speaker, a listener, both, or something else depending on the requirements of the narrative, the intangibles of cinematic pacing, or other considerations.

Two more ways to distinguish diegetic sounds are that they can be *external* or *internal.* **External diegetic sound** has a material source within the story world. Tires screech as a bank robber makes his getaway. These sounds, whether they're onscreen or offscreen, are external diegetic sounds. An **internal diegetic sound** originates in a character's mind. In *The Diving Bell and the Butterfly* (Julian Schnabel, FR/US, 2007) a man wakes up in a hospital after a catastrophic stroke. We see, from his blurry point of view, a woman peering over him and asking, "Can you hear me?" We then hear him reply, "I hear you." But no one in the room can hear him because the man is paralyzed and cannot speak. We are hearing his thoughts. This is an internal diegetic sound. Note that a potential for confusion is that onscreen and offscreen sound are one kind of "internal" and "external" sound and that internal and external diegetic sound are another kind. Take care to avoid mixing up these pairs of terms.

DIEGETIC SOUND AND TIME

Diegetic sounds can have different relationships to cinematic time. More pairs of distinctions flesh out this idea. There is *synchronous sound* and *asynchronous sound.* A hammer hits a nail. The sound occurs at the same instant at which the hammer is seen to make contact. This exact matchup between the sound's purported source and the sound itself makes this a **synchronous sound.** Suppose we see the hammer hit and hear the sound a second later. The discrepancy between the sound's apparent source and the sound itself makes this an **asynchronous sound.** In the early days of the sound era, which started in 1927, one option for storing sound was on spinning records that had to be mechanically synced with the film projector. The smallest technical problem could cause a loss of synchronization, and the resulting asynchronous sound would spoil the illusion, provoking laughter or anger. Films from later in the sound era sometimes incorporate asynchronous sound deliberately for comedic or other purposes, although this is rare.

There is also *simultaneous* and *nonsimultaneous sound.* **Simultaneous sound** occurs in plot time at the same moment it occurs in story time. Nearly all the diegetic sounds we hear in a film are simultaneous. The birdsong in both my hypothetical examples (onscreen and offscreen) is simultaneous. **Nonsimultaneous sound** is sound heard at a point in plot time that's different from the point at which it originates in story time. A child cries on his fifth birthday. We hear this cry in a scene in which the now-grown man plays golf. The crying is a nonsimultaneous sound. Such a sound might be motivated by a character's memory, or a film might justify the sound on other grounds (or, in a less unified film, maybe not at all).

Chapter 2 described a scene in *Written on the Wind* in which a character remembers a conversation from her youth (**2.12**). The moment in plot time at which these sounds are heard differs from the moment in story time at which they were made, so the sounds are nonsimultaneous. But note that there's a second way to construe this sound. We called this an example of subjective narration, as the woman is hearing these voices in her mind. This sound, then, is also an example of internal diegetic sound. These terms can overlap, and which one(s) you use may come down to what about the sound you think is important and how you're using it in your analysis. Regardless of which term you decide best fits this scene and your take on it, another that applies to this sound in *Written on the Wind* is that it's an example of a *voice-over*. A **voice-over** is speech delivered by one or more unseen speakers, who might be speaking in the past, as in this case, or from the future, as in a character-narrated flashback, or who might exist nowhere in the diegesis, as in some documentaries and TV commercials. (See **2.1–2.3** and **4.9–4.10** for more examples.)

Here's another example of nonsimultaneous sound. In *The Squid and the Whale* (Noah Baumbach, 2005) a boy walks home after running an errand. At the end of the first shot, we hear a door slam (**6.4**). The next shot starts a new scene, in which the boy, now home, says "I got it" (**6.5**). Some story time has elapsed between the shots, so this cut marks an ellipsis (see chapter 5). We hear the door slam while we're watching the boy still on his way home. The slamming sound occurs later in story time than when we hear it, so it's a nonsimultaneous sound.

Nonsimultaneous sound might seem to mean the same thing as asynchronous sound, and they do overlap, but they differ in degree and perception. If the sound and the image of its making are only slightly off, say a second or two—if the mismatch resembles, even if it's deliberate, a technical glitch—this is asynchronous sound. If the disparity makes you think not of glitches but of sounds moored in time as the characters experience it versus as we do—if it makes you think of narration—it is nonsimultaneous sound.

The sequence from *The Squid and the Whale* is also an example of a **sound bridge,** which is when diegetic sound from a scene overlaps the transition between it and an adjacent scene. Another example is in *Avatar* (James Cameron, 2009), when two characters share an intimate moment as they brace for an imminent attack (**6.6**). The next shot, starting a new scene, shows the rotors of the enemy aircraft roaring to life (**6.7**). The sound of these rotors is heard over the last several

6.4 *The Squid and the Whale.* At the end of this shot a door slam is heard.

6.5 At the start of the next shot we see the door we heard slam at the end of the previous shot.

seconds of the preceding shot of the lovers. Sound doesn't respect borders. It can spill across shots and scenes, and fill every corner of a movie theater auditorium. Here, a sound bridge dramatizes an invading force's spreading incursion into a peaceful world. Both of these sound bridges involve the sound from a scene being heard over the end of the previous scene. It's also possible for the technique to consist of diegetic sound carrying over from a scene into the one following.

Sound bridges can span an ellipsis, as in *The Squid and the Whale;* imply simultaneity, as in *Avatar;* and needn't indicate temporal relations

6.6 *Avatar.* In this sound bridge the menacing sound of enemy aircraft intrudes on an intimate moment.

6.7 The next shot begins a new scene and shows us the aircraft.

clearly or at all. In the documentary *Manufactured Landscapes* (Jennifer Baichwal, Canada, 2006) a handheld camera takes us down a narrow street in Shanghai and stops on a man cooking at an outdoor range (**6.8**). We hear a female voice say, "You see this open kitchen here . . ." The film cuts to a woman giving a tour of her spacious luxury kitchen as she finishes her sentence: ". . . actually was my garage" (**6.9**). The film has misled us into thinking the voice-over was referring to the street scene. Chapter 1 notes that similarities prime us to notice differences. Here they are extreme. By drawing a comparison between two kinds of

6.8 *Manufactured Landscapes.* A misleading sound bridge . . .

6.9 . . . encourages us to contrast two kinds of "open kitchen."

"open kitchen"—a parallel strengthened by red highlights in each setting —the film asks us to reflect on the gap between how the rich and the poor live in this teeming city. Whether this sound bridge links two scenes that are simultaneous or happening at different times is unclear.

Of the preceding terms, two that are often confused are *dialogue overlaps* and *sound bridges*. Remember that a dialogue overlap is dialogue only, and not some other diegetic sound as a sound bridge can be, and that it comes within a scene, while a sound bridge links two scenes.

DIEGETIC SOUND AND THE REAL WORLD

Some who have reflected on the medium over the years imply or state outright that the art of cinema lies exclusively in its visual qualities and that a film's sounds are mere recordings, copies of the real thing. This could hardly be less true. Sound in most narrative films is highly synthetic, constructed, and unreal. Sometimes a filmmaker does take care to make a sound approximate the way it would sound to a character in the scene. In *Butch Cassidy and the Sundance Kid* (George Roy Hill, 1969) a railroad employee has locked himself in a boxcar, and the bandits are trying to coax him to open the door so they can get to the safe inside. His refusals sound muffled, as they do to Butch and Sundance through the heavy door. Or imagine a scene in which a protagonist, hiding in a church, is trying to learn some secret information. Two monks pass behind a column just as one of them divulges it. The column obscures the sound at this crucial moment. The protagonist doesn't catch the information, and neither do we. (One might expect to find such a scene in a film in which the narration is restricted.) Both the *Butch Cassidy* scene and my hypothetical one are examples of a technique with a name that derives from "point-of-view shot," **point-of-audition sound,** which is diegetic sound that momentarily "locates us in the body of a character," meaning we hear it as the character does.

Dialogue handled in this way is uncommon, and most diegetic sounds are constructed according to principles that "fidelity" doesn't begin to describe. A film's soundscape is designed less with notions of realism in mind than with each sound's *narrative function* as the prevailing concern. Dialogue provides the most vivid example of this priority.

Dialogue in most narrative films has a high ratio of *direct* to *reflected sound.* **Direct sound** is sound that's coming straight toward a listener versus bouncing off walls and other surfaces. That kind of indirect, bouncing sound is **reflected sound,** which can be characterized by reverb, echo, and other "spatial markers" that can make a sound more realistic but also harder to understand. If a character is talking a good distance away from the camera in, say, a gymnasium, then making the speech quieter and increasing the reflected sound would make it more realistic; but if the character is saying things viewers need to hear in order to follow the story, then the dialogue will be altered to ease its comprehension. If you listen for it, you'll notice how unrealistically loud and clear dialogue sounds in most films.

Dialogue is so important to narrative comprehension that it's regularly rerecorded during postproduction through a process known as **automated dialogue replacement (ADR)**, under studio conditions in which the acoustics can be perfect and the sound controlled in precise ways. Other sounds, such as rustling fabric, footsteps, and clinking jewelry, are also routinely added later, created from scratch by craftspersons called **Foley artists** or selected from a library of stock sounds. Although some film practices and traditions over the years have captured "live sound" at the source and not manipulated it afterward, in an effort to bring viewers sounds that are as raw, unmediated, and real as possible, most commercial filmmakers today leave little to chance as they build up the soundtrack layer by layer, from the tiniest noises to the loudest explosions, controlling and modulating everything in between.

SOUND AND THE WHOLE FILM: A SCENE TRANSITION IN *TAKE SHELTER*

As you look at a film, remember to listen as well. Sound is part of the total package, and it interacts with all the visual elements you are observing. To illustrate, we'll close by considering the opening moments of *Take Shelter* (Jeff Nichols, 2011), in which a pair of shots hint at an ambiguity that structures the larger film.

At the beginning of the film a man stands on his front lawn as it starts to rain. He notices that the raindrops are oily and brownish yellow, a color motif in the film, as is a pattern of distant framings that show this man in his environment. He will come increasingly to believe that he's witnessing signs of an impending environmental catastrophe. But this man has mental illness in his family history, and the film's narration is constructed so that his uncertainty will be ours as well.

6.10 *Take Shelter*. Shower sounds from the next scene sneak in under the rain sounds in this shot.

6.11 Possibly, this sound bridge conveys the man's return to reality from his delusion, or it might simply link two times and spaces—an ambiguity that gestures toward the central question posed by the film.

We watch as he stands in the rain (**6.10**). The scene ends with a cut to the same man in the shower (**6.11**). The shots are linked by a graphic match, since in both shots water falls on him, and in both he's framed in a medium close-up—although his body orientation doesn't match across the cut. The shots are also linked by a sound bridge that is easy to miss. The downpour grows louder toward the end of the first shot, over which a different sound can also be heard—that of water hitting hard surfaces. This is sound from the next scene. The final note of the nondiegetic music that opens the film also carries across this cut, then ceases.

The film has just started, and viewers are only just settling into the story, so it probably slips past unnoticed that there are at least two plausible ways to interpret this cut. One is that it marks a simple ellipsis: he was on his lawn; now he's in the shower washing off that strange rain. A second way is that the images of the man on the lawn were totally subjective; they were inside the showering man's mind. Here I would place importance on the looseness of the graphic match. Had it been more emphatic—had the orientation of the man's body matched across the cut—the meaning of the transition would have been weighted more heavily toward the second interpretation, that we were watching the thoughts, and maybe hallucination, of a man in a shower. But the film won't tip its hand to what is really coming—global cataclysm or one man's descent into insanity—until the last scene (and even then it remains unclear to some viewers). The question of which interpretation to favor cannot be answered by looking and listening alone, and in this way the transition encapsulates and foreshadows the uncertainty that will haunt the entire film.

As you watch a film, remember to listen as well. How is sound interacting with the other major components of film style—mise-en-scène, cinematography, and editing? How is it shaping your sense of causality, time, and space? Do you hear any sound motifs? Listen and watch for ways these elements enter into relationships with each other and with the whole film.

Conclusion

A film is a network—a relationship of parts to each other and to the whole. If you understand how it all comes together, you will better grasp the singular moment. Attend to the moments, and you bring the big picture into clearer focus.

If you're interested in exploring such real-world issues as the effects of technology on our evolving sense of ourselves, and asking philosophical questions—like "What does it mean to be human?"—formal analysis can help you investigate how films explore and ask these same things. In *Blade Runner: The Final Cut* Special Agent Deckard envisions a unicorn (**2.13–2.14**). Later another cop, Gaff, leaves an origami unicorn for Deckard to find. Does Gaff know about Deckard's dream? If so, how? We learn that one of the human-like robots, or replicants, Deckard has been ordered to exterminate has been implanted with memories of a childhood she never had. Is Deckard's reverie, like Rachael's most personal memories, an implant as well? Deckard might be a replicant, too.

The film seeds related doubts in its viewers. We hear a character utter a line of dialogue, and later, a recording of it is played back with the wording and intonation slightly changed. Or maybe it's our memory of the line that is slightly off. Deckard looks at a snapshot Rachael kept because she believed it to be a picture of herself as a young girl with her mother. Deckard, who's falling in love with Rachael, stares at the photo, and just before the scene cuts away, the image stirs with movement. But it's only for a moment, and maybe our eyes were playing tricks on us, or our memory is now.

Eyes—windows of the soul, organs of visual perception and misperception—constitute a motif that runs through *Blade Runner* from nearly its first shot, when an extreme close-up of an eye fills the wide screen. When a genetic engineer beams with pride because he designed the leader replicant Roy's eyes, Roy tells him, "If only you could see what I've seen with your eyes." A robotic owl's eyes glow with a machine-like red light, as do Rachael's (and, in one shot, Deckard's). But Rachael, who mourns for her lost humanity, may be no less human than any other character in this film—including the protagonist we've been rooting for all along. What would it mean to our definition of *human* to accord her this status? On a rooftop Roy's life winds down as he cradles a dove in his hands. He tells Deckard about the wondrous things he's seen, then ruefully adds that "all those moments will be lost in time, like tears in rain." He dies and releases the dove. The symbolism is not subtle, but many viewers find it moving all the same.

This replicant has memories because he accumulated them through lived experiences, just like us. Does he have a soul, too? Is that what makes *us* human? The replicants are slaves in the dystopian future they inhabit. Where is the line separating us from the machines we increasingly depend on in *our* world, from pacemakers to subdermal hearing aids to thought-controlled prosthetic limbs to Google Glass? Thanks to technological advances that are constantly accelerating, this line keeps moving closer to what some regard as the very essence of human identity. As our smart phones become permanently glued to the palms of our hands—and smarter—we might ask whether this last border crossing has already happened, whether our future will liberate or irrevocably compromise us, and whether we're ready for—and can even guess—what the biggest consequences and implications of these transformations will be. Can smart phones, not yet invented when *Blade Runner* was made, figure in a reflection on this film's meaning? In a viewer-centered approach to the film, they can.

If you're interested in technology, race, gender, poverty, cities, sexuality, visual representations of premodern wars, cognitivist models of comprehension, screwball comedies, or Michael Haneke—whatever your orientation to a film—formal analysis can move you closer to ideas and questions that matter to you, help you develop claims that are grounded and convincing, and deepen your love of film art.

Practice noticing the elements and principles described in this book. Let this book become a dog-eared thing you throw in your bag when you know you'll be seeing a film later or working on your film essay. And keep watching films, both the kinds you've always loved and ones that are strange to you, films that will expand your horizons. And keep reading. Find writers who excite and inspire you and let them lead you to new film writers, subjects, and approaches. If you're watching a film on a Blu-ray or DVD and it seems baffling and opaque to you, see if there's a commentary track you can switch on; you might meet a guide who makes the film come alive for you and sends you hurrying to find more films from the same genre, movement, period, country, or director. Your relationship to the movies will change. Your ability to untangle and express your most complex and passionate thoughts about a film will grow, become more fully engaged, and bring you to new places.

INDEX

Page numbers for definitions are in **boldface.** Page numbers for figures are in *italics.*

development, 44, 46, 126
dialogue, 154, 159, 160–61
dialogue overlap, **154**, 159
diegesis, **50**
   See also diegetic sound
diegetic sound, **151**
   asynchronous, **155**, 156
   automated dialogue replacement
     (ADR), **161**
   dialogue, 154, 159, 160–61
   dialogue overlap, **154**, 159
   direct sound, **160–61**
   external, **154**
   Foley artists and, **161**
   form and, 161–63
   internal, 62–63, **154**, 155–56
   nonsimultaneous, 62–63, **155–56**
   offscreen, 105, **152–54**
   onscreen, **152**, 154
   point-of-audition, **160**
   realism and, 160–61
   reflected sound, **160–61**
   simultaneous, **155**
   sound bridges, **156–59**, 162
   space and, 152–54
   synchronous, **155**
   in *Take Shelter*, 161–63
   time and, 155–59
   See also voice-over
diegetic v. nondiegetic elements,
   50–52
difference and variation, 43
diffuse lighting, 78–79, *80*
digital color grading, **92**
digital compositing, *101*, **102**
direct sound, **160–61**
dissolve, **122–23**, *124*
disunity, 44–46, 53, *54*, 130–31
Diving Bell and the Butterfly, The,
   154
dolly shots, *112–13*, **114**, 117,
   118–19, *128*
dolly zoom, **97**

duration, **55**, 57
   See also long takes; screen
     duration
Dutch angle, **106**, *107*

edge lighting, **80**
editing, **121–22**
   axial cutting, 143–45, **147–50**
   composition and, 126–28
   contrasted with long take, 116
   cutting, **122**, *123*, 132–33, 142
   dissolve, **122–23**, *124*
   ellipses, *125*, **130–31**, 157, 163
   elliptical, **130–31**
   fade-out/fade-in, **122**, 123
   graphic match, **126**, *127–28*, 131,
     162–63
   in the camera, **121**
   overlapping, **131**, 145–46
   parallel editing, 53, **139**, 141–42
   in *Psycho*, 147–50
   rhythm and, 126, 129, 131–32,
     143
   space and, 129–30, 131, *149*
   time and, 130–31
   wipe, **123**, *125*
   See also continuity editing; Soviet
     Montage
editing in the camera, **121**
Eisenstein, Sergei, 3, 142–47
ellipses, *125*, **130–31**, 157, 163
elliptical editing, **130–31**
establishing shot, **134–35**
evaluating films, 32–33
expectations, 9–18, 30
explicit meaning, **20**, 22, 31
   in *Beauty and the Beast* (Disney), 27
   nondiegetic inserts and, 143
exposure, **90–91**, 92
external diegetic sound, **154**
extreme close-up, **111**, 166
extreme long shot, *109*, **111**
eyeline match, **136–37**

fade-out/fade-in, **122**, 123
fast motion, **92**
fill light, **82**
film genres, **11–13**
  See also individual genres
film interpretation, **18–19**, 165–67
  See also meaning
film narrative, **49**
  See also causality; narration; plot;
  story
film noir, 11, 55, 82
film style, **69**
  See also cinematography; editing;
  mise-en-scène; sound
Finding Nemo, 127
flashbacks, **55**, *56*
  causality and, 53
  motivation for, 34–35, 55
  plots and, 49–50
  subjective narration and, 34–35,
    62, *63*
  voice-overs and, 62, *63, 96,* 117,
    156
flashforwards, **55**, 61
focal lengths of lenses, 93–95
focus, 15–16, **97–99**
Foley artist, **161**
form, *xii,* 1, **7**
  "content" v., 8–9
  diegetic sound and, 161–63
  expectations and, 9–18
  in *La jetée,* 7
  in *The Sixth Sense,* 8, 44
  in *Star Wars: Episode IV,* 7–8
  in *Take Shelter,* 161–63
formal analysis, **1–3**, 7, 9, 19
  acting and, 83–84
  author intention and, 37–39
  of *Blade Runner: The Final Cut,*
    165–66
  evaluation v., 32–33
framing, **102**
  Academy ratio, *100,* **102**

aspect ratio, **102**
camera angle (high, low, straight-
  on), **106–8**
camera height (high, medium, low),
  106, *108,* 115
camera level (canted, level) , **106,**
  107
irises (iris-in, iris-out), **104**
offscreen space, **105–6**, 152–54
onscreen space, **104**, 152
sound and, 105, 152–54
split screen, **104**, 141–42
in *Take Shelter,* 161
widescreen, *100,* **102–3**, 104, 166
  See also camera distance; mobile
  framing
freeze-frame, 57, **93**
frequency, temporal, **57–58**
function, 34–36
  author intention v., 37–39
  dialogue and, 160
  props and, 76
  See also motivation

genre iconography, **12**
genres, film, **11–13**
  See also individual genres
Gone with the Wind, 54
Graduate, The, 79
graininess, **91–92**
graphic match, **126,** *127–28,* 131,
  162–63
Groundhog Day
  disunity in, 46
  explicit meaning in, 20
  implicit meaning in, 20–21
  motifs in, 40
  parallelism in, 23–24, 40
  referential meaning in, 20
  symptomatic meaning in, 23–24

hard lighting, 78, *80*
Henry V (1944), 44
high-angle shot, **106,** *107, 108*

meaning *(continued)*
    implicit, **20–22**, *128*
    referential, **19–20**
    See also symptomatic meaning
medium camera height, **106**, *108*
medium close-up, *110*, **111**, *114*, 162
medium long shot, *109*, **111**
medium shot, *110*, **111**
middle focal-length lens, **93**, *94*
mise-en-scène, **71**
    color in, 77, 126, 161
    computer generated imagery
        (CGI) and, 71, 73–74, 92, *101*,
        102
    costume and makeup, 76–77
    profilmic space and, 71
    props, **76**
    in *West Side Story*, 86–88
    See also composition; lighting;
        setting; staging; stylization
mobile framing, 111
    crane shots, *114*, **115**, 117
    motivation for camera movement,
        35–36, 117
    panning, *112*, **114**
    tilting, 45, *113*, **114**
    tracking shots, *112–13*, **114**, 117,
        118–19, *128*
    vertigo shots, **97**
    zooms, **94–97**, 114, 115
Montage
    See Soviet Montage
montages (Hollywood type), **142**
motifs, **40–43**
    in *Blade Runner: The Final Cut*,
        165–66
    camera distance as, 161
    in *Cat's Cradle*, 126, 129
    color as, 77, 161
    composition as, *85*
    costuming and, 77
    in *Groundhog Day*, 40
    props as, 76

    in *Secrets of a Soul*, 40–41, *42*, 76
    shadows and, 78
motivation, **35**
    for camera movement, 35–36, 117
    for characters, 59
    for flashbacks, 34–35, 55
    for lighting, 36–37, 44–45, *81*, 86
    for nonsimultaneous sound, 155
musical genre, 10, 82, 86–88
mystery film genre, 53, 60

narration, **59**
    curiosity and, 59
    in *Jeepers Creepers*, 67–68
    mystery films and, 53, 60
    objective, 65–66
    omniscient, **60–61**
    point-of-view shots and, 61–63,
        65–66
    restricted, **60–61**, 65–68, 160
    surprise and, 59, 60
    suspense and, 59, 60, 68
    unrestricted, **60–61**, 65–66, 68
    See also subjective narration
narrative, **49**
    See also causality; diegesis;
        narration; plot; space; story; time
Night and Fog, *128*, 131
No Country for Old Men, 130–31
nondiegetic inserts, **143**, *144*
nondiegetic sound and music, 142,
    151, 152, 162–63
nondiegetic v. diegetic elements,
    50–52
nonsimultaneous sound, 62–63,
    155–56
    See also sound bridges

objective narration, 65–66
offscreen sound, 105, **152–54**
offscreen space, **105–6**, 152–54
omniscient narration, **60–61**
180-degree system and line, **133–34**
    See also continuity editing

similarity and repetition, 39–43
    See also motifs; parallelism
simultaneous sound, **155**
Sixth Sense, The, 8, 44
slow motion, **92**
sound
    nondiegetic, 142, **151**, 152,
        162–63
    screen space and, 105, 152–54
    silence, 152
    See also diegetic sound; voice-
        over
sound bridges, **156–59**, 162
Soviet Montage, 74, *75*, 132, **142**
    attractions in, 142–43
    axial cutting in, 147–50
    Battleship Potemkin, 144–46,
        147, 150
    compared to continuity editing,
        147–51
    Eisenstein, Sergei, 3, 142–47
    jump cuts in, 143–45
    nondiegetic inserts in, 143, *144*
    overlapping editing in, 131, 145–46
    Strike, 143, *144*
space
    diegetic sound and, 152–54
    editing and, 129–30, 131, *149*
        (*see also* continuity editing)
    offscreen, **105–6**, 152–54
    onscreen, **104**, 152
    plot, **58**
    screen, **58**, 104–6, 152–54
    story, **58**
special effects, **100**
    digital compositing, *101,* **102**
    matte work, *100,* **101–2**
    rear projection, **100–101**
    superimposition, *63, 91,* **100**
speed of motion, 92–93
split screen, **104**, 141–42
Stagecoach, 134–40

staging, **82**
    acting and performance, 83–84
    aperture framing, *85,* **86**, *140*
    deep-space, **84**, 98–99
    in *Letter from an Unknown
        Woman,* 117–20
Star Trek (2009), *108*
Star Wars: Episode IV, 7–8, 50, *100*
Star Wars: Episode V, 11
story, **49–50**
    duration, **57**
    narration and, 59
    space, **58**
straight-on angle shot, **106**, *108*
Strike, 143, *144*
studio v. location shooting, 73–74, *75*
style, **69**
    See also cinematography; editing;
        mise-en-scène; sound
stylization, **72**, *73*
    acting and, 83–84
    costume and makeup and, 76–77
    realism v., 72
subjective narration, 61–66
    in *Blade Runner: The Final Cut,*
        64, 165
    flashbacks and, 34–35, 62, *63*
    internal diegetic sound and, 154,
        155–56
    in *Take Shelter,* 161–63
superimposition, *63, 91,* **100**
surprise, **14**
    in K-Fee Turbodrink TV commercial,
        15–16
    mystery films and, 60
    narration and, 59, 60
    in *Pulp Fiction,* 17–18
suspense, **13**
    in *Indiana Jones and the Temple
        of Doom,* 14–15
    in *Jeepers Creepers,* 68
    long takes and, 115
    narration and, 59, 60, 68

DESIGN AND COMPOSITION: SANDY DROOKER
TEXT: 10/14 BERTHOLD AKZIDENZ GROTESK
DISPLAY: BERTHOLD AKZIDENZ GROTESK
PREPRESS: EMBASSY GRAPHICS
PRINTER AND BINDER: QUALIBRE